AF480780

MUIRGEN'S CAROUSEL

MUIRGEN'S CAROUSEL

The Hope of Return

A Libretto by M. Turandot

MUIRGEN'S CAROUSEL: THE HOPE OF RETURN

Published by Miragwyn Books Manakin-Sabot, Virginia

www.mturandotauthor.com

This is a work of fiction. Names, characters, places, and incidents are either the product of the author's imagination or are used fictitiously. Any resemblance to actual persons, living or dead, events, or locales is entirely coincidental.

Library of Congress Control Number: 2026907862

ISBN: 979-8-9994617-3-5 (Hardcover)

ISBN: 979-8-9994617-4-2 (Paperback)

First Edition: May 2026

Set in Sabon.

Printed in the United States of America.

Cover and interior layout design by M. Turandot. Select editorial elements and theatrical language refinement were developed through a collaborative process with the assistance of AI tools, finalized with the author's creative discernment and care.

To Donald Louis Jean—my beloved reed in the wind.
For the music of Cork and Clare, for keeping the tempo
of my heart steady through every season,
and for being the anchored center
that empowers my carousel to spin.
This libretto is for you,
with love
from the quiet harbor.

*When we become whole, the world reveals its
design—cycles within cycles, harm and
harmony bound in the same turning. What once
felt mute begins to speak in pattern, and
reverence teaches us where to stand.*

—M. Turandot

TABLE OF CONTENTS

FOREWORD

Stories about the sea have always been stories about ourselves. We project our longing onto the tide, our fears onto the deep, our hope onto the horizon. *Muirgen's Carousel* was born from that ancient conversation between the human heart that wants safety and the elemental truth that asks us to listen.

This work began as a series of questions: What if environmental crisis is not only a political failure, but a spiritual one? What if the storm outside is inseparable from the storm within?

Fionn's journey follows a pattern many of us inherit: a quiet harbor built from silence, endurance mistaken for strength, and a lifetime of unspoken grief. When the sea finally speaks through a goddess, a selkie, a banshee, a child made of memory—it is not to punish, but to remind him of the part of himself he abandoned.

The world of this play moves between myth and modernity, between satire and sincerity, between collapse and renewal. Its form embraces cycles: the turning of the tide, the turning of the Carousel, the turning of a life that has stalled but can still begin again.

If the story has a single belief, it is this: When we become whole, the world becomes possible. The sea hums beneath every denial, waiting for us to hear her. When we finally do, the storm becomes an opening—and the hope of return arrives like dawn.

—M. TURANDOT

A Note on Form

Muirgen's Carousel is written as a mythic musical, moving fluidly between the human and the elemental. Chorus, sound, and imagery function not merely as background, but as memory, conscience, or the living presence of the sea itself.

Transitions are intended to be musical and visual rather than strictly literal, inviting an imaginative, non-proscenium approach to staging. Not all images require psychological interpretation; some exist solely to establish rhythm, reverence, and emotional terrain.

The work balances humor, satire, and gravity, acknowledging both the creative and destructive forces of nature. Its form embraces cycles, patterns, and return—asking not for mastery over the elements, but for the courage of coexistence.

This libretto is offered not as a finished monument, but as a living map. Like the tide it describes, it is subject to change, meant to be amended by the hands that hold it and the voices that sing it in years to come. It belongs to the 'quiet harbor' of the reader's imagination as much as to the stage. If, like a message in a bottle, it finds a home in some future century, let those who find it treat it as a conversation—one that began in a small room in Virginia and continues wherever the sea is heard.

Dramatis Personae

Fionn Murchadh - Tenor / Baritone

A fisherman hardened by loss and denial. His quiet resilience masks an unresolved childhood trauma and a self-made emotional exile. His journey toward listening—to the sea, to memory, to himself—forms the heart of the story.

Muirgen - Soprano

The sea personified—ancient, elemental, and watchful. She appears first as a fierce judge and later as a mirror of compassion. Her voice carries the weight of tides, memory, and consequence. [1]

Lí Ban - Mezzo-Soprano

A Selkie and the human-scaled embodiment of Muirgen's tenderness. Once close to Fionn, she represents the love, vulnerability, and forgotten promise he cast aside. She bridges myth and humanity, surface and depth. [1]

Banshee - Mezzo-Soprano/ Alto

A spectral truth-teller with comedic bite and operatic wail. Part conscience, part omen, she punctures denial with razor-sharp humor. Her cries are the sound of collective grief made impossible to ignore.

Minister of Flow - Baritone / Bass

The local bureaucrat and a polished political spinner who treats crisis like a press opportunity. Charming, evasive, and desperate to control the narrative, he becomes both a foil and reluctant ally to the Banshee.

Harbormaster - Baritone / Character Tenor

The overworked, exasperated authority of the docks—practical, frazzled, and perpetually outmatched by circumstance. Comic ballast with moments of surprising clarity.

CLERK - Tenor

A timid bureaucrat caught between truth and fear. His confession becomes the catalyst for Fionn's deepest reckoning.

CROW CHORUS

A sharp-eyed, sardonic Greek Chorus of three to five townsfolk. Half-avian, half-prophetic, they echo the town's denial, amplify Muirgen's judgment, and provide rhythmic, darkly comic commentary.

CHILD OF THE SEA - Soprano

A bioluminescent, haunting presence. They speak in whispers and melody, holding memories the living have forgotten. They guide Fionn toward recognition and integration.

TOWNSFOLK / ENSEMBLE

Fisherfolk, pub regulars, bureaucrats, market vendors, dockworkers, and townspeople. Their shanties, arguments, humor, and fear embody the community's collective denial—and their potential for change and renewal.

FISHERMAN

A speaking part within the Ensemble.

CHILD

A non-speaking part, representing Fionn's younger brother, whose drowning is the source of his guilt.

[1] *Lí Ban and Muirgen are two aspects of the same mythological entity, representing the human and mythic spheres, respectively. Muirgen is the personification of Lí Ban's Anima or Mythic Self, visible to Fionn only at moments of spiritual crisis and confrontation.*

Setting and Time

Setting:

A small industrial harbor town on the coast of Ireland. The action primarily takes place on the docks in the harbor square, and by the shoreline, dominated by the rusted, decaying, half-submerged frame of Muirgen's Carousel.

Time:

Present day, during a period of ecological crisis and political apathy. The final image shifts slightly outside of conventional time.

Musical Numbers

PRELUDE

PRELUDE

The Ocean Remembers

SETTING: The vast, mysterious Ocean at night. There is no physical set—only darkness and light.

LIGHTING: The stage is saturated in a very deep blue-green. This is not moonlight, but a color suggesting the pressure and mystery of the water itself (BLUE-GREEN TWILIGHT).

MUSIC CUE: As the lights come up, the audience hears the continuous, low sound of surf and the distant, mournful calls of whales. This is overlaid by a very soft, relentless pulsing in 6/8 time (the heartbeat motif), in a low drone like a whale's heartbeat. The music must establish a sense of immense depth, both physical and emotional.

STAGE PICTURE: Against the darkness, a single image is slowly brought into focus: a child standing alone at the water's edge (This figure will later echo FIONN MURCHADH's drowned brother). The image is fleeting, immediately followed by an almost impossible vision projected onto the backdrop: a shimmer of constellations on the waves and dolphins arcing in golden light, all slowly appearing.

(The CHORUS—a small group of 2-3 voices in simple flowing gray—enters slowly, drifting toward center stage like a bank of mist.)

CHORUS (In a low, rhythmic chant; following the 6/8 pulse) They deliver the Prelude poem, *The Ocean Remembers*, building the dramatic stakes and the sense of tragedy.

The waves once danced with sapphire light,
Now darkened, burdened–drowning white.
Where children ran, their feet now wade,
Through waters ghosted, beauty frayed....

(The pulse quickens slightly; the voices rise in a minor-key resonance.)

CHORUS (Final words of the poem are spoken with great weight, slightly accented by a minor chord in the orchestra): *Éist! Labhraíonn an fharraige…*

[THEMATIC NOTE: These Irish lines establish the mythic wound and set the moral stakes: the ocean once pure, now poisoned, still remembering.]

(The stage picture and the heartbeat motif hold for a brief, pregnant moment before the transition to Scene 1.)

[MUSICAL MOTIF NOTE: This slow 6/8 heartbeat motif will appear in every act to establish the emotional arc: sacred, mournful, and finally hopeful. A call to wake, rise, and to set it free.]

"THE OCEAN REMEMBERS"

CHORUS
(spoken or sung in free rhythm)

The waves once danced with sapphire light,
Now darkened, burdened–drowning white.
Where children ran, their feet now wade,
Through waters ghosted, beauty frayed.

The tide still sings, but hoarse, unheard,
Its voice entangled in plastic words.
The kelp still sways, the fish still flee,
Yet shadows choke the sacred sea.

Once, dolphins played in silver glow,
And rivers kissed the depths below.
Once, foam was salt, not poison's trace,

Once sea and sky held no disgrace.

But now, the pipes release their ghosts,
A silent curse upon the coasts.
Their whispers coil in briny breath,
A spell of ruin, a song of death.

Yet listen–listen–hear it well,
The ocean speaks, it weaves its spell.
It calls to those who still can see,
To wake, to rise–to set it free.

For tides can turn, and wounds can heal,
If hands will build and hearts will feel.
The waters wait, the waves implore–
Will you restore what was before?

CHORUS
(in Irish, quietly)
Éist! Labhraíonn an fharraige.
Mara cuimhníonn sí.
Filleann na taoide arís.
Cosnaímid ár bhfarraigí, ár dtodhchaí.
Cuir an fharraige saor arís.

Listen! The sea speaks.
The sea remembers.
The tides return.
Let us protect our seas, our future.
Set the ocean free again.

(A single child steps forward, listening. The light of
dawn begins to rise behind them. The heartbeat merges
with a faint, melancholy waltz rhythm and the faint
metallic creak of a carousel turning once in the fog.)

(A slow dissolve–from mythic ocean to harbor.)

(The ocean's low hum continues.)

*(Lights warm toward dawn, fading into gray-gold.
Distant gulls cry. Harbor bells ring.)*

*(The sound of the sea transforms into metallic–rusted,
circular–the decayed CAROUSEL creaking as it turns once.)*

*(The melancholy waltz rhythm becomes a broken
calliope jangle.)*

(A half-sunken carousel frame glints with rusted mirrors.)

(The child's silhouette fades; the harbor town takes its place.)

(The smell of the harbor enters.)

*(The CAROUSEL's jangling tune begins–then abruptly
snaps into grinding metal and finally grinds to a sudden
stop. The low hum sustains.)*

(The harbor is now fully present.)

(HARBORMASTER and BANSHEE enter.)

HARBORMASTER
(Dryly, staring at the CAROUSEL)

Look at this thing. Still turning.

BANSHEE
(Cackling, then sharply)

The only thing spinning 'round here is the rot.

ACT ONE

SCENE 1

What's One More Drop?

SETTING: The scene is the Harbor Docks at a coastal town, just as dawn begins to break. The harbor is a place of industry and slight neglect. Nets, barrels, and fish crates are scattered haphazardly everywhere. A thick, low fog clings to the water's edge, shrouding the details of the bay.

STAGE PICTURE: At the far edge of the dock, half-submerged in the rising, polluted tide, stands the decaying, rusting frame of a CAROUSEL. Its bright paint is chipped and its mechanisms are seized—a poignant, broken symbol of past joy. The town itself is still half-asleep, indicated by the occasional cries of gulls, the insistent chiming of bells from a distant steeple, and the sporadic, metallic sound of dripping pipes near the water.

ATMOSPHERE: The air is heavy and still, carrying a faint, pervasive stench—not the clean smell of the sea, but something processed and industrial.

The scene begins with the opening sounds of crowd banter from the local townspeople and dockworkers, which quickly leads into the rousing Ensemble Shanty that sets the pace for the morning's work.

(The HARBORMASTER enters from stage left, pausing to breathe deeply. BANSHEE stands near the CAROUSEL frame.)

HARBORMASTER

And a top 'o the morning to ye too, Banshee. *(Breathes deeply)* Smell that? Progress.

BANSHEE
(Sniffs, souring)

Smells like progress went off three days ago. Like a promise left out in the sun.

HARBORMASTER

Nonsense. That's industry—rich, briny, employable.

BANSHEE

If the tide gets any higher, you'll be employable as a lifeguard.

HARBORMASTER

Let it rise! Bit of sea never hurt a seafaring town.

BANSHEE

Aye, till the sea starts knocking and asks for rent. And Lí Ban is a demanding landlord.

(A fisherman trudges past with buckets of sludge instead of fish.)

HARBORMASTER

What's one more drop, eh?

BANSHEE

That's how you drown—one drop at a time.

(She hums a low note. Others join in—murmuring rhythm becomes song.)

"WHAT'S ONE MORE DROP?"

ENSEMBLE
(Verse 1)
Patch the boat, ignore the leak,
The forecast's fine for one more week!

We've bailed before, we'll bail again—
The sea's our oldest next of kin.

CROWD
(call-and-response)
What's one more drop? (Just one!)
What's one more wave? (For fun!)

BANSHEE
(sardonic solo line)
When the sea keeps score, she'll use your lungs.

ENSEMBLE
(Chorus)
What's one more drop in an endless sea?
A little denial keeps spirits free!
Pour another pint, patch another tear,
If the world's still spinning—we're in the clear!

(The crowd ends the shanty with a final, messy, drunken cheer / clash of instruments. The final chord is loud, manic, and messy. The energy of the town instantly dissipates. They scatter back to work.)

(The lights are still bright. All sound cuts, leaving a sudden, shocking silence. The stage action freezes for a beat. The wail - high, piercing, and full raw grief is heard).

(SFX: BANSHEE WAIL - HIGH, SUSTAINED, PURE TONE.)

CROW CHORUS

The truth has a nasty pitch.

BANSHEE
(Adjusting her ghostly clipboard, comic deadpan.)
That was a perfectly executed act of collective denial. Give yourselves a hand.

(Three CROWS scattered among the set, remain center-stage. They stop their movements simultaneously. They perform a sharp, synchronized head tilt as if catching a frequency no one else hears.)

(The HUM / Pulse of the Sea: A low, sustained, subtle sub-bass frequency enters the theatre soundscape (the heartbeat from "Listen". This sound is not a song; it's a feeling.)

CROW 1

The rhythm's off.

CROW 2

Too fast. Too loud. Too cheap.

CROW 3

The Sea Warrior can't hear the song he's singing.

CROW 1

But she hears his silence.

(The CROW CHORUS dissolves into the fog. The low HUM sustains. The lights shift, focusing on FIONN MURCHADH, who has been standing frozen mid-action.)

HARBORMASTER
(To FIONN, completely unaware of the Crows)

Your turn, lad—sing something optimistic before the Minister arrives.

(FIONN sighs, tips his cap, and begins his intimate, myth-activating beat).

SCENE 2

The Net Is Empty

SETTING: The same Harbor Docks as the previous
scene, though the focus is now tighter, the light concentrated.

LIGHTING: The lighting narrows to a single, lonely
spotlight on the central figure.

MUSIC CUE: The music transitions from the rousing
Ensemble Shanty to the quieter, deeper sound of the 6/8
Heart Motif—the low HUM of the sea sustained
beneath the music. This music, first heard in the Prelude,
now underscores FIONN's emotional state.

STAGE PICTURE: FIONN MURCHADH is alone in
the center stage area beneath the spotlight. This is the
first time he is truly alone with the "sea's heartbeat"
sound. He is trying to drown out the ache of his
loneliness and grief by using humor and song. His
posture attempts to be cheerful and lighthearted, but the
mask of his performance is visibly thin.

*(The scene begins with FIONN delivering his solo
monologue—a wry fisherman's ballad full of humor that
quickly shades into profound melancholy.)*

"THE NET IS EMPTY"

FIONN *(Solo)*
(Spoken-sung / light humor)
Funny thing about nets—you spend your life
untanglin' 'em. Then one day you haul up
nothin' but your own reflection.

(He laughs; the laugh catches in his throat.)

But it's fine. The sea's just playin' hard to get.
She'll cough up a haddock when she's in the mood.

(He hums a teasing sea-shanty tune.)

(Verse 1,Comic Shanty Tone)
I tossed my hopes to the deep blue ground,
Said "fetch me fortune, big and round!"
She sent me boots, a tire rim,
And half a message, sinkin' dim.

(Chorus 1, Wry Humor)
The net is empty, the beer is not,
The sea's gone shy, the day's gone hot.
If faith's a fish, she slipped the line—
But hope still swims, and hope is mine.

FIONN

(He chuckles, sips from a flask. The wind hushes.)

(Spoken-sung)
What's one more drop, right? Just a little
denial to keep the boat afloat.

*(Tone shifts. The "Whisper Melody" enters the
orchestration subtly.)*

(Verse 2)
I once could hear her heartbeat low,
A pulse that told me when to row.
Now all I hear's a plastic chime—
A ghost in time, a ghost in time.

*(Note: This echoes the Crow Chorus line "can't hear the
song he's singing.".)*

(Lights dim to blue; distant crows echo the final phrase.)

(Chorus 2, earnest reprise / latent grief)
The net is empty, the sea won't speak,
She's holdin' breath for what we seek.

I dream her voice will call me home—
Till then I cast, alone, alone.

(FIONN is on his knees, nets pooling around him; a single feather lands in the ropes—silent foreshadowing of LÍ BAN (The Selkie) and the Net of Light.)

FIONN *(mid-verse callback-spoken then sung)*

(He pulls up a bit of trash from the water.)

"What's one more drop," she teased and grinned,
Till drops became a flood within.

(He discards the trash. A single feather lands in the ropes—silent foreshadowing of LÍ BAN. He notices it, but quickly dismisses it.)

(Music fades down, leaving only the sustained low HUM.)

SCENE 3

Sea You Later

SETTING: The Pier at dawn. The scene is quiet, the gulls being the dominant sound of the waking town.

STAGE PICTURE: A slick, dark trail of seaweed runs from the edge of the surf to a heap of sealskins piled on the Pier. FIONN remains center stage, kneeling by his fishing net and muttering to himself as he works. The single feather he dismissed in the previous scene is still tangled in the ropes—a constant, visual reminder of the ocean's mystery.

MUSIC CUE: The low, sustained HUM (the sea's heartbeat) continues beneath the scene, punctuated by the rhythmic, soft sound of the waves breathing in 6/8 time. The faint sound of the "Listen" motif is audible, underscored beneath the natural sound of the wind, suggesting the ocean's silent observation.

ATMOSPHERE: The action begins with BANSHEE quietly reappearing (or emerging from the shadows), observing FIONN in silence during the prelude. She holds the stage briefly before she will exit, leaving FIONN alone with the presence of LÍ BAN, though she is invisible to him. Only the BANSHEE can see her.

BANSHEE
(Quietly, watching the water)

Ye smell that, Fionn? Sea's holding her breath.

(There is an uncanny silence / tension).

FIONN

Aye. Probably offended by the Minister's cologne.

BANSHEE

No. Something uncanny. She's tired of talking to herself.

(BANSHEE gives a knowing, theatrical laugh and exits, leaving FIONN alone.)

FIONN
(Working, muttering)

Stitch the hole, patch the past. If only guilt took twine.

(He pulls the rope; it snaps. He sighs.)

(SFX: A SOFT, DELIBERATE SPLASH NEARBY.)

LÍ BAN
(Offstage)

You dropped something, land-walker.

FIONN

Oi! Who's there? If it's another tourist feedin' crisps to the seals—

(The Selkie, a shimmering figure rises from the surf, dripping, near the CAROUSEL frame, wrapped in a tangle of nets. Light catches her silver-green skin beneath the fabric. This is LÍ BAN.)

LÍ BAN

Don't flatter yourself. I've better taste in snacks.

FIONN
(Blinking, half-amused)

You're... indecently mythical.

LÍ BAN

And you're indecently landlocked.

FIONN
(Turning back to his work, grumbling)

Thought I was alone in my bad luck.

LÍ BAN

Luck? You call this luck? I borrow your rubbish for one midnight swim and wake wrapped like a trawler's dream. This yours?

(She holds up a bit of the torn net that broke in Scene 1.)

FIONN
(half-amused)

You should try paperwork. That's where real drowning happens.

LÍ BAN
(Smiling, sarcastically)

Ah, humor. A defense mechanism—how human.

(She wrings water from her hair; it falls in spiral patterns glowing faintly blue.)

FIONN

You're glowing. Is that contagious?

LÍ BAN

Only if you remember what awe feels like.

(They study each other; the orchestra slips into a lilting jig rhythm.)

"SEA YOU LATER"

LÍ BAN
(Verse 1)

I came for a breath of the air you steal,
For a glimpse of the world you forgot was real.
You net the waves, you bottle the foam—
You've left the sea with no way home.

FIONN
(Verse 1)

Oh wise sea-maid with rhymes so neat,
You steal my fish and call it sweet!
If love's a wave, I'll build a dam—
I'm tired of drownin' who I am.

LÍ BAN
(Verse 2)

You cast your nets and call it love,
But love's a wave—you stand above.
You shout her name, yet plug your ears—
I've seen such men for years and years.

FIONN
(Verse 2)

I came for a catch and a cup of tea,
Not sermons from amphibious royalty.
If guilt were fish, I'd be rich today—
So what brings you up my way?

LÍ BAN
(Chorus)

Sea you later, sailor brave,
Your nets are empty, your pride's a grave.
But if you'd trade one jest for a tear,
You might just learn to listen here.

*(She gestures toward the surf; faint whispers echo
"Listen... listen....")*

(Dialogue Interlude)

LÍ BAN

Your net's for fish, not feelings.

FIONN

Both wriggle, both stink, both escape.

LÍ BAN

Then you've never held one proper.

(She takes his hands; tiny droplets shimmer like stars.)

FIONN

Is that the wind?

LÍ BAN

It's memory. The sea keeps copies.

(Tempo softens; they circle each other.)

(Bridge)

FIONN

You talk like a tide with a tale to sell.
I've paid in salt; I know it well.

LÍ BAN

Then pay attention, love—that's free.
The storm's already billing thee.

(They share a laugh, tension melting.)

(Duet - Playful Counterpoint)

FIONN

Stay on land, you'll catch a cold.

LÍ BAN

Stay at sea, you'll grow too old.

(Bridge)

FIONN

You talk in riddles, kelp-for-brains.

LÍ BAN
At least mine still remember rains.

(They circle each other; the music shifts from jig to 6/8 waltz.)

BOTH
(Final Refrain / Chorus: The Romantic High Point)
Sea you later, maybe never,
Tide can't promise calm forever.
If we meet when hearts are clear,
Hold your breath—I'll draw you near.

(Waterlight rises around them, then retreats. Feather drifts by unnoticed.)

Sea you later, fate's begun,
Two stubborn hearts, one rising sun.
If laughter can't save what's true and deep,
We'll wake the sea before she sleeps.

(Music fades with gull cries; they stand side-by-side, watching the horizon. Distant rumble hints at Muirgen's first omen to come.)

[Closing Action - Tone Change / Plot Point - Inciting Incident]

FIONN
If you were real, you'd have the sense to run from this town.

LÍ BAN
If you were listening, you'd have heard me say—I can't.

(She rapidly sheds her shimmering, half-seal cloak / coat, which is caught in FIONN's net. She dives into the water, vanishing instantly. Only the cloak remains.)

FIONN
(To the sea, quietly, looking at the cloak in conclusion)

Sea you later, then.

> *(Act One swells, then fades into the harsh, bureaucratic rhythm of the next scene: "Forms in Triplicate." The cloak is the new emotional anchor.)*

SCENE 4

FORMS IN TRIPLICATE

SETTING: The Harbor Office. This is a small claustrophobic space that barely functions. The room is dominated by a stack of soggy paperwork and several desks mounted on rolling casters, suggesting constant, clumsy reorganization. The bureaucracy is announced by a large, official-looking sign that reads: "Department of Aquatic Accountability - Because the Tide Waits for No One."

STAGE PICTURE: The HARBORMASTER, the MINISTER OF FLOW, and BANSHEE are positioned in the office, giving the impression of a group of cogs grinding against each other—they occupy the space like a malfunctioning clock. The movement and tension are high, setting up the impending quick rhythm of the scene.

MUSIC CUE / ATMOSPHERE: The scene is a bureaucratic musical farce rooted in physical comedy and quick patter song. The dialogue is set up to have a fast, overlapping rhythm, immediately signaling a shift in pace and tone from the previous scenes. The tempo is brisk and frenetic.

(The scene begins with the HARBORMASTER attempting to take charge of a chaotic situation.)

(Sharp, percussive sound (like a rubber stamp hitting a desk or a loud typewriter ding) to immediately kill the romantic atmosphere.)

HARBORMASTER

Right, next order of business: the Sea Complaint Form B-Seventeen.

BANSHEE

What's the complaint?

HARBORMASTER

The sea's too wet.

BANSHEE

File it under "irreversible."

MINISTER OF FLOW

Excellent. Progress! Transparency! Accountability!

HARBORMASTER

Minister, the public's nervous about the pipes.

MINISTER OF FLOW

Nervousness is patriotic energy. I'll rebrand it.

BANSHEE

You'll rebrand the smell? Good luck, love.

"FORMS IN TRIPLICATE"

MINISTER OF FLOW
(pompous)

Regulation is salvation,
Paperwork prevents damnation!
If the sea should rise, we'll keep her calm—
With ink, approval, and bureaucrat balm!

HARBORMASTER
(counter-melody)

Sign here, sign there,
Two copies for the mayor!
We log each wave, we stamp each shell—
Efficiency keeps the kingdom well!

BANSHEE
(dry interjection)

And when it floods, we'll drown in style—
File by file by file.

(Music turns into patter at double tempo; they shuffle papers like tap dancers.)

ALL THREE *(patter section)*

Form A, Form B, Form C, D, E!
Cross-reference in Section Three!
When chaos knocks, we'll set a meeting,
Minutes first—ignore the bleeding!

(They stamp papers in sync - percussive comedy. Crows echo the rhythm outside.)

(Bridge - dialogue over music)

BANSHEE

Minister, perhaps the sea doesn't fill out forms.

MINISTER OF FLOW

Then she's in violation of the Clean Paper Act!

HARBORMASTER

Shall I send her a fine?

BANSHEE

Send her a poem. She's more likely to pay attention.

> *(The music stumbles; brief silence. Thunder murmurs.*
> *BANSHEE tilts her head, hearing distant crows.)*

BANSHEE

Hear that? She's laughing.

MINISTER OF FLOW

Nonsense. That's optimism rattling the pipes.

> *(Finale Tag - return of chorus)*

ALL *(reprising)*

Regulation! Celebration!
Keep those forms in circulation!
If we drown today, it's no mistake—
We'll document each splash we make!

> *(Lightning flicker; papers scatter like snow.)*

> *(The MINISTER OF FLOW strikes a proud pose as*
> *thunder cuts the lights.)*

SCENE 5

PROGRESS AFLOAT

SETTING: The Harbor Square and Docks. The square has been hastily decorated with bright bunting and banners celebrating the illusion of change. The most prominent banner reads: "A Cleaner Tomorrow - Today!"

STAGE PICTURE: A raised podium has been constructed from stacked barrels, where the MINISTER OF FLOW presides. Scattered around the podium, the TOWNSFOLK gather. The HARBORMASTER and FIONN are among them, wearing expressions that range from skeptical to half-hopeful. The BANSHEE is situated near the crowd, having been co-opted or "roped into communications" (likely translating the official nonsense for the less-informed), observing the scene with a wry, knowing air.

MUSIC CUE / ATMOSPHERE: The scene immediately bursts into a big ensemble, bureaucratic musical farce. The sound of a distant, sharp whistle blows once. VOICE (Offstage or from the Harbor Rigging) (A high-energy, traditional nautical shout) "Heave away!" The MINISTER OF FLOW attempts to sell a hopeful future to the town, using language rooted in full brass-band irony. As the lights snap up brightly, the music slams in. A marching band (or the sound of one) provides a rhythmic, insistent beat with marching bass drum and snare drum. THE TOWNSFOLK crowd the stage, chanting slogans and clapping, building a sense of forced escalating enthusiasm.

(The scene begins with the MINISTER OF FLOW addressing the crowd in an opening banter spoken in a fast, overlapping rhythm, leading directly into the ensemble number.)

MINISTER OF FLOW
(projecting over the brass, with manic energy)

Citizens! Friends! Future investors in sustainability!

BANSHEE
(Translating to crowd, dryly)

He means "hold your nose and smile."

MINISTER OF FLOW

Today we celebrate a re-route revolution! Our pipes will flow—*(beat)*—PROGRESSIVELY!

(The crowd breaks into hesitant cheers as the brass flourishes into a triumphant, slightly dissonant "button.")

CROWD
(Hesitant cheers)

Hooray…?

HARBORMASTER
(Wiping sweat, leaning to a TOWNSFOLK / FISHERMAN)

I tell you, we're running in circles with these forms.

FISHERMAN

Circles? Mate, we're not running. We're just stuck on the same old ride.

HARBORMASTER

What ride?

FISHERMAN
(Gestures vaguely toward the half-submerged Carousel)

Muirgen's Carousel. You pay your shilling, you sit on the painted horse, and you go round and round. The music is cheap, the scenery never changes, and you end up right back where you started.

FIONN
(A sharp, quiet line)

And the horse is rotten underneath.

MINISTER OF FLOW
(Clapping his hands, oblivious to the dialogue)

A pipe line here, a drain divert! We call this Progress Afloat!

"PROGRESS AFLOAT"

MINISTER OF FLOW
(Verse 1)
Raise your banners, ring the bell,
We've harnessed hope—and a pleasant smell!
A pipeline here, a drain divert,
Efficiency makes the future flirt!

CROWD *(call & response)*
Progress! Afloat!
Keep our worries in a note!
Progress! Afloat!
Ship the truth and rock the boat!

HARBORMASTER *(aside)*
If progress leaks, I'll take the blame—
Long as I can spell its name.

(Verse 2 - MINISTER OF FLOW & BANSHEE Counterpoint)

MINISTER OF FLOW
I've balanced budgets, soothed the press,
Reduced the ocean's... damp excess!
Our numbers shine, our graphs ascent—

What could possibly offend?

BANSHEE
(counterline)
You promise charts that sparkle neat,
But something's rotting 'neath your feet.
When truth erupts, don't call it fate—
Call it overdue update.

*(They circle one another; the brass grows cheeky,
Sousa-meets-klezmer.)*

(Bridge - Comic Dance Break)

*(Paperwork twirling like confetti. The CROWS join,
forming a marching band with feathered batons.)*

CROW CHORUS
(shouting over music)
Caw! Regulation! Celebration!
Caw! Evacuation—soon!

(Laughter; thunder rumbles under the rhythm.)

FINAL CHORUS - FULL COMPANY
Progress Afloat, hooray, hooray!
Tomorrow's clean if you pay today!
We patch the leaks with grand intent!
Success is ninety-nine percent consent!

BANSHEE *(overlap)*
Or one percent common sense.

(Crowd cheers; thunder rolls louder, lights flicker.)

MINISTER OF FLOW
(To crowd, shouting)

See? Even the heavens applaud—!

*(Lightning flashes; the MUIRGEN's crow shadow
crosses the stage.)*

(Coda; tone darkens.)

(Music cuts mid-trumpet note. A single feather drifts down. Silence.)

CROW CHORUS *(whisper)*

Caw... audit incoming.

(Blackout)

SCENE 6

MUIRGEN's FIRST OMEN

SETTING: The Harbor Square and Docks. The aftermath of the rally is visible, with confetti, wet papers, and sea mist swirling in the air. A few TOWNSFOLK remain onstage, sweeping up the detritus.

LIGHTING: The bright, high-energy lights of the previous scene dim rapidly to a twilight blue, deepening the sense of mystery and transition.

MUSIC CUE: The musical freneticism ends abruptly. The brass-band sound fades out slowly and completely, leaving only the bellows and hiss of the wind as a base. A low, ominous HUM begins, pulsing rhythmically with a heartbeat rhythm (part cello, part sustained wind instrument), instantly signaling the return of the mythic tension.

STAGE PICTURE: As the stage darkens and the soundscape changes, crows begin to wheel overhead. Their cries stretch and harmonize into a sound that is both eerie and melodic. At this moment of unsettling silence, feathers fall from above—a visual sign of the incoming omen. The HARBORMASTER is seen sweeping, attempting to restore order, while the BANSHEE and MINISTER OF FLOW react to the sudden shift in atmosphere.

(The scene begins immediately following the dispersal of the rally, with the HARBORMASTER expressing his desire for "quiet progress.")

HARBORMASTER
(To himself, sweeping)

Wouldn't mind a bit of quiet progress for once…

(The broom catches a single black feather. He frowns.)

BANSHEE
(Looking up)

Do ye hear that?

MINISTER OF FLOW

What?

BANSHEE

The silence. It's... organized.

(Thunder murmurs. The papers lift into the air lightly.)

"MUIRGEN'S OMEN"

CROW CHORUS
(Soft, rhythmic whisper)

Caw... balance... caw... balance...
The ledger is open...

(A column of light cuts through the mist; inside it, a tall
shadow—the suggestion of wings, not yet the full
Muirgen. Her voice comes from everywhere and nowhere.)

MUIRGEN (offstage or amplified)

I am the ledger of the sea.
When laughter drowns too loud,
I count the bubbles.
When ink runs, I read the stains.

(The crowd freezes; the MINISTER OF FLOW drops
his clipboard. The ink from it seeps outward like dark water.)

MUIRGEN (cont.)

You balance books in triplicate—
I balance souls in tide and bone.
The tide does not negotiate!
The deep does not file a form!

(The light flares, then extinguishes. Feathers rain down like ash.)

(Coda.)

(FIONN steps forward, alone in half-light, catches a falling feather.)

FIONN
(Quietly)

Storm's changing her tone.

(A single crow caws. Blackout. Cue into pub scene.)

SCENE 7

Why I Don't Swim

SETTING: The Harbor Pub. The room is characterized by sticky tables, low laughter, and an atmosphere that is loud, chaotic, and cynical. This bustling intimacy serves as a sharp contrast to the quiet intensity of FIONN's conversation.

STAGE PICTURE: The BANSHEE is situated behind the bar, a silent but observant presence who is the only character able to interact with the mythical realm. LÍ BAN is seated directly across a table from FIONN. Her presence is slightly ethereal as she is part of FIONN's imagination. She is the only person in the room who is neither drinking nor engaging in the pub banter until FIONN speaks to her. The other TOWNSFOLK ignore her or seem to look straight through her.

DRAMATIC TENSION: This scene is defined by a deep ambiguity: the AUDIENCE should be left to wonder whether FIONN is speaking to a genuinely troubled young woman or to the mythical embodiment of his guilt and tragic past.

MUSIC CUE / ATMOSPHERE: The background of the pub is thick with low, cynical laughter and loud chatter. Outside, a faint gull cry is heard, a small, lonely reminder of the sea. The scene centers on the intimacy of FIONN's conversation with LÍ BAN.

(The scene begins with LÍ BAN's first line, delivered across the table to FIONN.)

LÍ BAN

You live on the water, yet you never touch it. Even the gulls bathe once a day.

FIONN

Aye, well, I did my swimmin' early in life. Got my certificate in terror and pneumonia.

LÍ BAN
(Chuckling)

What—did the sea insult your boots?

FIONN

Something like that. She bit back, once. Left a storm inside me that never quite settled.

BANSHEE
(Quietly, polishing a glass behind the bar, pretending not to listen.)

That's what she does to the ones she wants to keep.

(A rare moment of validation.)

FIONN

Don't start with curses and destinies. It's simpler: water went bad. I drank too much of it. Now it drinks me, bit-by-bit.

LÍ BAN
(Turns serious, leaning in slightly)

A Sickness?

FIONN

Just a reminder. Belly protests every time I forget who I owe. The sea and I—we've an unsettled tab.

(Beat: Laughter bubbles loudly from another table, releasing the tension. The BANSHEE moves to center stage behind the bar, raising a mug.)

BANSHEE
(To the room, voice cutting through the noise.)

Well, here's to debts paid late and lives half-salted! You'll never be whole, but you'll always be safe!

(She slams a mug down. The crowd cheers loudly. The moment passes, but the shadow of the "unsettled tab" lingers on FIONN's face.)

SCENE 8

SETTING: "The Drunken Buoy", the town's pub. The room is a high-energy, cynical den where the wooden floor is visibly slick with seawater. The lighting is provided by string lights that flicker like bioluminescence, suggesting a warped, unnatural beauty.

STAGE PICTURE: The BANSHEE acts as the host of the evening, overseeing the chaos. FIONN, the HARBORMASTER, and various locals crowd the tables, holding pint glasses that appear to hold more microplastics than foam, serving as a potent visual joke about the town's environment. A jukebox hums with static in the corner. The MINISTER OF FLOW is positioned somewhere nearby, basking in the reflected glory of the town's temporary distraction.

CHARACTER ACTION: FIONN is present but distracted. He furtively touches the single feather he keeps tucked in his pocket, a silent reminder of the omens and the conversation in the previous scene.

MUSIC CUE / ATMOSPHERE: The scene is a sea-shanty cabaret of denial and dirty humor. The atmosphere is loud, boisterous, and rooted in a desperate attempt to ignore the town's decline.

(The scene begins with the BANSHEE kicking off the cabaret, initiating the high-energy ensemble number.)

BANSHEE

Evenin', sinners of the shoreline! Drink special tonight: The Oil Slick. Half stout, half despair, garnished with a bit of existential dread!

(Crowd cheers)

HARBORMASTER

What's the ABV on existential dread?

BANSHEE

Depends how guilty ye feel after swallowin'.

(Laughter. The band kicks into a slow jig.)

"PINTS AND PLASTIC"

ENSEMBLE
(Verse 1, Raucous)
The sea gave birth to every fish,
And we returned the favor—
We feed her lids and bottle bits,
To thank her good behavior!

CHORUS

Pints and plastic, cheers and fate,
If the tide looks thick—must be great!
Raise your glass to the glossy foam,
Where every straw finds a happy home!

FIONN
(Verse 2 - The Conscience Leaks)
(Soft, reflective, solo over the ENSEMBLE undercurrent)
I cast my nets and heard her cry,
A sound too deep for drinkin'.
The sea's gone hoarse, the gulls fly shy,
And still we toast, not thinkin'

ENSEMBLE
(Overlapping, raucous)
Drink up, lads, the pipes may burst,

But drownin's better than a thirst!

(Bridge - FIRST OMEN (THE SNAP) - BANSHEE's spoken interruption)

BANSHEE

(Sharply, slamming a pint down)
Quiet—listen. She's hummin' again.

(Music cuts; faint underwater Act Two, from "Omen" returns.)

HARBORMASTER

Just the fridge.

BANSHEE

Fridges don't breathe.

(Silence—crow caw outside.)

ENSEMBLE

(Final Chorus - defiant laughter into fear)
(Forcing cheer, rushing back into song)
Pints and plastic, sink or swim,
If the end is near, we'll toast to it!
The sea can't judge our merry din—
Pour another round and let her in!

(Thunder booms; glasses vibrate. Lights flicker. The crowd freezes mid-toast.)

BANSHEE
(soft)

She's already in.

(A brief musical bridge shifts the crowd into comic frenzy.)

BANSHEE
(Spoken)

You know it's bad when even the mermaids order bottled air.

FIONN
(To himself, quieter)
Aye... but the air's gone briny too.

(He rubs the feather he found; the lights shift slightly bluer.)

(He shakes his head, then forces a loud, cynical laugh to drown the thought.)

BANSHEE
(Sharply, sensing the change in FIONN)
(To CROWD)

Alright, you daft souls. Quiet—listen! Ye want to sing about it? A proper anthem for the age of plastic! On three—new anthem! "Oh Shite... It's Real!"

"OH SHITE, IT'S REAL"

*(Tempo doubles; the music turns into a desperate,
cynical singalong to drown out the fear. The mood is manic.)*

*(LÍ BAN with BANSHEE harmonizing and possibly
FIONN chiming in halfway through)*

BANSHEE
(Verse 1, channeling LÍ BAN's voice)
I swam through kelp and coral bright,
Where silver fins would gleam at night,
But now the sea tastes oddly thick—
Like sewage soup and plastic brick.

(BANSHEE, as herself, deadpan)
A dolphin's corpse just winked at me.
I think it died ironically.

CHORUS
(All, manic, upbeat)

Oh shite, it's real, the sea's gone grey,
And fish now swim the other way!
The tide rolls in with sick perfume,
A whiff of bleach, despair, and doom!

We warned ye once, we warned ye twice,
But now the ocean's full of wipes!
So clap your fins and kick your heel—
Oh shite, my friends, it's real.

FIONN
(Verse 2, Grumbling, but swept into the manic tempo)

Me net pulled up a traffic cone,
A nappy and a garden gnome.
The haddock left without a word—
They mutinied and joined a bird.

BANSHEE
(as LÍ BAN)

I held a council with the squids—
They've packed their sacks and moved to Madrid.

CHORUS
(All, stronger harmony, faster)

Oh shite, it's real, the pipes all leak,
And I've got rashes on my beak!
The kelp's turned plaid, the seals all cough,
And someone flushed their Spanx right off!

So raise a glass, but not from here—
This pint's been marinating fear!
We're cursed with greed and clueless zeal—
Oh shite, me loves, it's real.

(Bridge)

BANSHEE
(mournfully, slightly pulling back the tempo for a beat of truth)
They paved the shore, they dammed the stream,
They bottled up the selkie's dream.
And now we howl, and now we sing,
But no one listens to a thing.

BANSHEE
(as LÍ BAN - passionately)
Unless we shout and make a scene—
With glitter signs and tambourines!

FULL CAST
(Final Chorus)
(Maximum manic energy, kazoos optional)
Oh shite, it's real, no time to stall,
The sea's alive—and she's pissoff, y'all!
She's rising up to flood your shoes,
And wash away your tabloid news!

So plug the pipes, pick up your trash,
Before she gives her final splash!
It's not a drill, nor a surreal spiel—
Oh shite, sweet Earth, it's real!

BANSHEE
(Final Catastrophe)
(Softly, mocking)
(Slamming a pint down; the mug catches the faint underwater heartbeat motif.)
"What's one more drop," ye sing, ye clowns—
till one more drop is all ye drown.

(She hushes them. Music is reduced to a frantic, distorted rhythm.)

FIONN
(unconsciously echoing in his own lyric)
The net is empty... but my hands still ache.

ENSEMBLE

(Forcing cheer, quieter)

We're cursed with greed and clueless zeal—
Oh shite, me loves, it's real!

*(Thunder booms, closer this time, and glasses vibrate.
Lights flicker violently. The crowd freezes mid-toast.)*

BANSHEE

(Soft, final line for the scene)

She's already in.

*(Blackout on the pub scene. Only the low heartbeat
HUM remains. Leading directly to the "Audit of Souls.")*

SCENE 9

The Storm Remembers

SETTING: The Drunken Buoy suddenly transforms.

LIGHTING: The lights dim dramatically to a solitary blue-gray wash.

STAGE PICTURE: As the lights dim, the chaotic laughter and sound of the pub dissolve completely into the noise of the surf. FIONN freezes mid-movement, standing alone, half-drunk, and swaying. The stage focuses entirely on him and the rapidly changing atmosphere.

MUSIC CUE / ATMOSPHERE: The low, pulsing heartbeat drum that underpins the mythic scenes begins to swell into the sound of crashing waves. This shift is underscored by the low, sustained HUM of the sea. Eerie, the distinct sound of a child's whistle—the tiny tune heard earlier in the shanty—echoes faintly across the stage, pulling FIONN into a painful memory.

(The scene begins with FIONN, swaying and speaking to himself, lost in the immediate, hallucinatory memory.)

FIONN
(swaying, speaking to himself)

The sea owes me nothing... nothing at all.

(He sets his mug down. The glass ripples as if moved by an unseen tide. He still clutches the feather.)

(SFX: A sudden, sharp gull cry transforms into a deafening thunder roll.)

(PROJECTION: Silhouette of two boys on a pier; ropes whip in the wind.)

YOUNGER VOICE
(Offstage, echoing, panicked)

FIONN! Look, I can stand where the boards are broken!

FIONN
(Gasping)

No, come back—!

> *(He lunges; the projection shatters into bubbles. The
> sound shifts underwater—muffled heartbeat, distorted bell.)*

> *(He flails, hands reaching through the invisible water.
> Blue light strobes; his body stiffens, reliving the drowning.)*

FIONN
(Gasping)

I saw him sink, but I didn't see him go.

Only the rope—

and the taste—

metal and salt—

The world shrinking to a throatful of dark.

> *(He falls to his knees. The sound of water drains away,
> replaced by a soft child's hum—the same tune, now
> sung by the Child of the Sea.)*

CHILD OF THE SEA
(Offstage, gentle)

You kept my storm inside you.

That's why it hurts when you forget.

> *(Light catches on his face; he looks upward, tears
> indistinguishable from sea-spray.)*

FIONN

Then forgive me, little one.

I only meant to breathe.

> *(He exhales; a single bubble of light rises and vanishes.*
> *The heartbeat resumes its human rhythm. The pub noise*
> *slowly fades back in—life continuing.)*
>
> *(The blue light holds, isolating FIONN. This is the*
> *moment before the final Act One song.)*

SCENE 10

THE AUDIT OF SOULS

SETTING: The stage achieves a visual merge of the Drunken Buoy pub and the Harbor. The walls of the pub appear to peel away or dissolve, dramatically revealing a horizon of dark, churning water and violent lightning. The floor is now littered with the physical evidence of the town's neglect: piles of discarded nets, soggy papers, and pint glasses.

STAGE PICTURE: The scene explodes into chaos. FIONN is alone onstage, still reeling from the vision of "The Storm Remembers." The MINISTER OF FLOW bursts onto the stage, drenched and frantic, waving sodden documents—the epitome of bureaucracy undone by nature.

MUSIC CUE / ATMOSPHERE: The scene starts in a state of chaos rising. The heartbeat motif is now a full, urgent, thunderous drum rhythm. The lights flicker violently as the soundscape becomes terrifying: the instruments of the brass band detune themselves, their notes morphing into a chaotic wail that sounds like sirens. This is the moment of Muirgen's true arrival and the start of the first, devastating flood.

(The scene begins immediately with the chaotic entrance of the drenched MINISTER OF FLOW.)

MINISTER OF FLOW

We have a minor oversight! The tide's filed a complaint!
(Fast/Patter)
Section four, sub-clause B.
The surge is not a guarantee!
I have the forms, I have the files.
The flood is stretching out for miles!
It's just a clerical glitch in the moon's rotation,
A slight misprint in the sea's taxation!

HARBORMASTER
(To the frozen crowd)

Just like the Minister said—perfectly right! It's just a bit of damp!
No need to ruin the bunting!

BANSHEE
(To the audience, dryly over the ticking music)

You paid for balcony seats—hope you can swim.

> *(Laughter is immediately drowned by thunder. The
> HUM is now a continuous, deep drone.)*
>
> *(Floorboards heave; a gush of brown water shoots
> upward from a pipe fracture. This is the Policy Failure
> from "Progress Afloat.")*
>
> *(MUIRGEN's Judgement)*
>
> *(Lightning flashes, illuminating the stage. In the mist, a
> tall figure appears—MUIRGEN—her cloak of black
> feathers alive, her voice resonant and amplified, as if
> speaking from the sea floor.)*

"BALANCE THE BOOKS"

MUIRGEN
(Spoken)

I am the line between profit and prayer,
The ledger of salt in the Minister's hair.
Every drop counted, each oath on file—
Your balance sheet's been short a while.

You counted coins, I counted cries,
The sea kept score in salt and bone—
Now every debt comes crashing home.

> *(Wings unfurl; black feathers spiral outward as
> projections of waves climb the walls.)*

Balance the books, balance the sea,
Each drop a ledger written by me!

*(Under this line, the underlying orchestra quotes the
main "What's One More Drop?" melody, slowed and in
a minor key—the audience subconsciously hears the first
song's irony and the town's denial transformed into judgment.)*

You borrowed breath, you spent it wild—
Now the sea collects her child.

CROW CHORUS
(frantic, echoing)
We tally the waste, the greed, the guff—
The books are full—enough's enough!

MINISTER OF FLOW
Now let's be calm—there's no need for fright!
Our infrastructure's sound—well, mostly—tonight!
If the ink hadn't run, we'd be perfectly right!

BANSHEE
(Dry)
The pipes just screamed, love. That's not applause.

MUIRGEN
You drown in denial.

(Bridge - The Fisherman's Appeal)

*(FIONN steps forward, leaving the net with LÍ BAN's
cloak tangled in it. He looks up at MUIRGEN.)*

FIONN
Take me, then. I've dragged enough ghosts in my nets.
You can count in storms, I count in loss—
my brother, my boat, my own crossed cross.

MUIRGEN
(Softening slightly)
You confess, yet you don't listen.
When you can hear without excuse, I will hear you.

*(She lifts her hand; the water projection rises around
FIONN, but does not touch him. It holds him in an
uneasy spotlight.)*

MUIRGEN & ENSEMBLE *(Finale)*
Balance the books, the page is turning,
Ash to foam and hope to yearning!
When ink meets blood, the truth reveals—
What drowns the world is what it feels.

*(Water projection bursts over the back wall; strobe
flashes simulate lightning. All townspeople freeze in a
tableau of panic and awe.)*

MUIRGEN
(Spoken over a fading drum drone)

The audit is open.

Act Two will show who pays.

*(A single, final black feather falls onto FIONN.
Thunder rolls into absolute silence. Blackout.)*

*(Intermission cue: The HUM of the heartbeat continues
faintly in the dark as the curtain drops—an auditory
thread leading the audience from terror to the satirical
wreckage of Act Two's opening scene.)*

INTERMISSION

ACT TWO

SCENE 1

WHAT FLOATS?

SETTING: The Main Stage, immediately following the ACT ONE Blackout. The set is visibly damaged and flooded, reflecting the impact of the burst pipes and the storm surge. The stage floor is slick with water, emphasizing the danger and slapstick potential.

ATMOSPHERE / SENSORY DETAIL: The air is thick with brown-gold ripples through mist and the pervasive, overlapping scent / sound of salt, sewage, overlapping alarms, and gulls.

STAGE PICTURE / ACTION: The stage is littered with debris. A pipe bursts center stage *(SFX: CREAKS, SLOSHES, SUDDEN WHOOSH)*, sending jets of water spraying through the previously bright, promotional "Progress Afloat?" banners. The CROW CHORUS enters, avoiding the debris in slapstick choreography.

[MUSIC CUE: The opening is an introduction spoken in chaotic, overlapping rhythm, immediately signaling the start of a high-energy ensemble number built on panicked denial.]

CHOREOGRAPHY: The Chorus uses mops as partners and buckets as drums.

SOUND: The music drops the melody and focuses on a heavy, clattering percussion beat—think metal pipes clanging and rhythmic water splashes. The percussion should sound organic and metallic, not just a standard drum kit.

GAG: The "Garden Gnome" salute happens here, punctuating the final beat of the dance break before the duet begins.

(The scene begins with the HARBORMASTER attempting to restore order amidst the chaos.)

HARBORMASTER
(Wiping sewage from his cap)

Everybody stay calm! *(beat)*

Does anyone know how to swim?

CROW CHORUS
(Chanting in canon)
The pipe! The pipe! The pride took flight!
Now truth leaks out in broad daylight!
They dodge debris in slapstick choreography.

MINISTER OF FLOW
(Still trying to smile)

Just a minor setback—

A demonstration model!

BANSHEE

Congratulations, love.

Your policies finally made a splash.

"WHAT FLOATS?"

MINISTER OF FLOW
(Verse 1)
It's not a flood, it's a liquid event!
A subsidized surge of a coastal descent! The
sewage is merely a vintage bouquet,
To welcome the tourists who've come for the day!

ENSEMBLE
(Verse 2)

(This should shift from the Minister's solo into a full-
blown, manic Ska-Punk rhythm.)

Buckets and mops, we're knee-deep in proof,
The tide is inside, and it's trashing the roof!
From bottle to diaper, the detritus spins—
Our sins, my friends, have sprouted fins!

(Stage gag: a garden gnome floats by; FIONN fishes it out and salutes it.)

(Verse 3 - FIONN & LÍ BAN duet fragment)

LÍ BAN
You see what you've done?

FIONN
I see what we've drowned.

LÍ BAN
Then dive for the living, not ghosts underground.

FIONN
(Clutching a floating keg)
I paid for the round! I'm keeping the foam!

LÍ BAN
(Pulling his arm)
The plastic is heavy! It's dragging you home!

FIONN
It's shiny! It's sturdy! It's all that I've got!

LÍ BAN
It's salt in your lungs and a heart full of rot!

(They plunge offstage as lights cut to strobe; chaos continues.)

(Bridge - MINISTER OF FLOW & BANSHEE)

MINISTER OF FLOW
Can we spin this as a cleansing initiative?

BANSHEE
(singing)
Spin it, dear, till the whirlpool grins—
Then let it swallow your original sins!

(Comic tango echo of "You Promise / I Wail," setting up the next scene.)

FULL COMPANY *(Finale)*
What floats will rise, what sinks will tell,
The sea keeps score, she tolls the bell!
Our fortunes bob in the undertow—
Clean hands, dirty water—oh, don't you know!

(Blackout as the music turns minor; projection of storm funneling into silence.)

SCENE 2

You Promise / I wail

SETTING: The Harbor-Office Pressroom, immediately following the flood. The room is messy and visibly damp. The walls are covered in blaring slogans like "Progress Afloat!" Mops, buckets, and soggy, crumpled documents litter the floor.

STAGE PICTURE: The MINISTER OF FLOW rehearses his talking points before a mirror (or a microphone stand), while the BANSHEE initially haunts the space, invisible to him. The staging of the mops and microphones should allow them to double as the tango props.

MUSIC CUE / ATMOSPHERE: The introduction is spoken rhythmically leading directly into a comic tango that physically exposes the contradiction between political spin and harsh reality. The Tango Vamp begins with a distinct musical texture: bass and bandoneon are undercut by the faint, unsettling whistle of the wind.

(The scene begins with the MINISTER OF FLOW's attempt to spin the flood damage.)

MINISTER OF FLOW

Water's up two inches, but so's the polling. The people love a flood—as long as it's televised.

BANSHEE
(Invisible, mocking echo)

Televised! Sanitized! Sterilized truth for breakfast.

MINISTER OF FLOW
(Startled)

Who's there? Another intern?

BANSHEE
(Appears, clipboard glowing)

Your conscience in heels, love. Don't mind me—carry on spinning.

(Tango vamp begins: bass + bandoneon + faint whistle of wind.)

"YOU PROMISE / I WAIL"

MINISTER OF FLOW
(Verse 1)
I promise the pipes are resilient and clean,
The finest the coastline has ever seen!
A minor eruption? A seasonal quirk—
We'll patch it with slogans and paperwork.

BANSHEE
(counter-verse)
You promise, you promise,
But pipes have a pulse.
You squeeze them for profit
Till honesty gulps.

(Refrain 1 - Together, tango step)

BANSHEE

You promise—

MINISTER OF FLOW

— I manage!

BANSHEE

You polish—

MINISTER OF FLOW

— You damage!

BOTH

We dance on a drain love, We tango with sludge.

BANSHEE *(Verse 2)*

You sold the sea her own reflection,
Bottled hope and called it "correction."
You whisper reform with a mouth full of foam—
I scream the truth, but you call it tone.

MINISTER OF FLOW
(Verse 2, Overlapping)

I lead with intent and efficient repair,
Our nation demands a minister's flair!
If sewage should seep, it's a technical glitch—
The tide, not the policy, made the switch.

(Bridge - dance break)

(They circle, mops as partners.)

(BANSHEE flicks dirty water toward his shoes.)

BANSHEE

Careful, darling—truth stains silk.

MINISTER OF FLOW

Better silk than sackcloth, dear.

(Beat of stillness. Their eyes lock. Humor softens.)

BANSHEE

You used to sing at rallies, remember? Before you learned the key
of denial.

MINISTER OF FLOW

And you used to listen before you... well, screamed.

BANSHEE

Touché

(Refrain 2 - quieter, bittersweet)

> You promise the moon
> While the tide takes the town.
> I wail for the ones
> Still too proud to drown.
>
> We're perfect together—
> Disaster and spin—
> You promise, I wail,
> And the sea breathes us in.

(Music swells; they finish the tango pose, half-embrace, half-stalemate. Applause cue.)

SCENE 3

Council of Myths

SETTING: A half-submerged meeting room. The furniture visually confirms the flood damage: chairs float, and clipboards bob on the surface of the water, which is mid-thigh deep on the characters. A dripping sign attempts to maintain normalcy, reading: "Transparency in Action." This space is the physical and bureaucratic fallout of the previous scenes.

STAGE PICTURE: FIONN, LÍ BAN, the MINISTER OF FLOW, and the CROW CHORUS delegates are all present. The CROW CHORUS is physically active, slapping the puddles with their wings to emphasize their chaotic interjections.

MUSIC CUE / ATMOSPHERE: The scene begins with chaotic, overlapping dialogue as the HARBORMASTER attempts to call the meeting to order. The dialogue quickly establishes a rhythmic, farcical conflict between the characters' different priorities.

The scene begins with the HARBORMASTER trying to maintain command amidst the chaos.

HARBORMASTER

Right! Order! By authority vested in… whoever's still buoyant!

CROW CHORUS

Caw! Order! Order!

(They slap puddles with wings.)

MINISTER OF FLOW

Please note for the record: the current situation is fluid.

BANSHEE

So's your leadership, love. Mostly backwash.

LÍ BAN

The sea sent warnings! Did none of you read the foam?

FIONN

I read the waves. They spelled "idiots."
(Laughter beat from audience.)

"GUILT BY THE GALLON"

(Comic patter)

ENSEMBLE
(rapid-fire counterpoint)

(Incorporating the debris and slapstick from "What Floats?")

Buckets and mops, we're knee-deep in proof,
The tide is inside, and it's trashing the roof!

Who dumped the sludge?
Not me! Not me!
It's a matter of jurisdiction / maritime ambiguity!

Whose bright idea rerouted the drain?
That'd be progress—please define the term again!

CROWS
(Interjecting in barbershop style)
Guilt by the gallon, guilt by the ton,
Everyone pointing their hose at someone!

HARBORMASTER
(Spoken over music)
All in favor of a subcommittee on absolution—say "Aye"?

CROWS
Caw! Aye!

BANSHEE

Eye roll noted!

(Middle section - debate turns absurd)

MINISTER OF FLOW

We need a rebranding campaign. Something hopeful—"Resilient Rising!" No—"Harbor Strong!"

LÍ BAN

How about "Sorry!" Short, catchy, truthful.

FIONN

Print it on buckets. We'll sell redemption by the liter.

BANSHEE

Finally, a policy I can scream about.

(She gives an operatic wail; a ceiling tile falls into the water.)

HARBORMASTER

That's coming out of maintenance!

CROW CHORUS
(Imitating meeting minutes)

Item 12: structural integrity compromised by emotional honesty.

(Laugh break.)

(Bridge - moment of clarity through laughter)

FIONN

Look at us—arguing while the sea's still in the room.

(Everyone pauses. Water licks the edge of the table.)

LÍ BAN

Maybe the council's meant to listen, not talk.

BANSHEE

Good luck filing that motion, love.

> *(Beat of stillness to a soft harp riff cue that will grow
> into the next scene, "What Remains When We Stop Blaming.")*

FIONN

I'll second it anyway.

> *(Tag - Exit into duet)*

HARBORMASTER

Meeting adjourned on account of existential flooding!

CROWS
(Chant)

Minutes submitted, souls uncollected—Next agenda item: self-reflection!

> *(Lights dim. BANSHEE and MINISTER OF FLOW
> linger, exchanging a quiet, comic-tender glance as
> FIONN steps into moonlight for the duet.)*

> *(All clear the stage quickly except for the lingering few.)*

SCENE 4

Guilt by the Gallon (Reprise)

SETTING: The flooded meeting room, the same as the Council of Myths.

STAGE PICTURE: All characters (BANSHEE, HARBORMASTER, FIONN, LÍ BAN, the MINISTER OF FLOW, and CROW CHORUS) are still present. They are dramatically frozen mid-argument, standing in the thigh-deep water.

MUSIC CUE / ATMOSPHERE: The frantic energy and laughter of the Council are converted into a quiet, reflective space needed for the Heart of the Sea vision that follows. A short musical reprise softens the tone, with the bandoneon from the earlier number creeping back in—now slower, in a minor key, and wistful. This brief musical snippet leads directly into the number "What Remains When We Stop Blaming".

"GUILT BY THE GALLON (REPRISE)"

(Instrumental Intro)

(Low strings plus the earlier patter rhythm at half-tempo; crows beat wings softly for percussion.)

(Ensemble lines - half-spoken, half-sung)

BANSHEE
Guilt by the gallon... we've measured enough.

MINISTER OF FLOW
The spin's gone flat and the tide's turned rough.

HARBORMASTER

My forms are soaked, my pen won't write.

CROW CHORUS

Record the truth in moonlight.

(Music pauses - water drips in rhythm.)

(FIONN's solo - bridge to next song)

FIONN

(Softly)

If we're done with blaming, what's left to save?
Maybe just breath... and the brave.

(He takes a step forward. Light shifts from amber to silver.)

(Underscore gathers quietly.)

(Harp and low drone enter; tempo slows to 6/8. The melodic line of the reprise resolves on the opening chord of the next scene.)

(All others fade into shadow as FIONN is left alone.)

SCENE 5

The Heart of the Sea

SETTING: The aftermath of the Council.

STAGE PICTURE: The stage empties into darkness, revealing only faint bioluminescent ripples on the water's surface. FIONN drifts in, half-conscious, holding his broken net. From beneath the water, the CHILD OF THE SEA appears, rising with a childlike glow and shimmering in translucent blue.

MUSIC CUE / ATMOSPHERE: The soundscape is built on haunting simplicity: a low heartbeat pulses beneath the stage, fading into distant whale calls. The core melody, "Listen," is formed by a single harp string plucked repeatedly, creating a wordless melody.

The reprise in the scene before does not resolve. Allow the silence to establish itself fully before the first harp note. The audience must feel the room change temperature.

(The scene is a spoken-sung sequence.)

CHILD OF THE SEA
(Echoing, gentle)

You spoke of mending, but you forgot to mend yourself. The sea cannot heal what you refuse to hear.

FIONN

Then teach me.

> *(He kneels; water ripples outward, forming concentric circles projected onto the backdrop.)*

"LISTEN"

CHILD OF THE SEA
(Sings - ethereal soprano)
Listen where silence becomes air.
The sea remembers every tone
That mercy sang when you were alone.

*(FIONN's shadow joins the CHILD OF THE SEA's,
synchronized in the water.)*

FIONN
(Spoken)

I thought I heard my brother once—in the foam. Maybe it was
you.

CHILD OF THE SEA

He lives in the undertone. All voices return, if you let them.

(Instrumental Bridge)

*(Harp and strings rise; projections of old toys, nets,
shells drift across the backdrop. MUIRGEN's crow
feather floats through the light; the CHILD OF THE
SEA catches it.)*

CHILD OF THE SEA
(Whispers)

Carry this to her. She's waiting to forgive herself, too.

(Feather glows; FIONN pockets it. The waterlight dims.)

(Final Line - shared, sung)

BOTH
Listen.

*(Sound fades to a single, resonant heartbeat - the cue for
the next scene.)*

SCENE 6

THE CLERK'S FEAR

SETTING: The area near FIONN's boat.

STAGE PICTURE: The scene takes place during a brief, false calm. FIONN is the eye of the storm, quietly trying to fix his boat. The CLERK rushes in, his atmosphere frantic and bureaucratic, providing a stark contrast to FIONN's stillness. The CLERK is soaking wet and trembling with fear (terrified, not dramatic), his clothes sticking to him, and he clutches a saturated binder.

(The scene immediately follows the ethereal "Heart of the Sea Vision".)

CLERK

Fionn! Fionn Murchadh! I… I'm sorry, I have to tell you. It's not just the big fish, not just the harbormaster. It's the paper.

FIONN
(Tiredly)

I don't care about your permits, Clerk. The tide is coming in past the dock.

CLERK

But you're on the list! That last permit—the one that allowed the factory to dump directly into the old channel—the signature is forged, but it's your license number. They used your name to finalize the order.

FIONN
(Stares at the CLERK, jaw tight.)

I never signed that.

CLERK
(Wringing his hands, trembling)

No, but you looked the other way when the others did their deals! You kept your head down! You chose the quiet harbor—and they used your silence as their signature. You didn't pull the trigger, Fionn, but you helped them load the gun!

> *(The CLERK drops the binder and runs off. FIONN is left alone.)*

SCENE 7

The Quiet Harbor

SETTING: The Harbor Docks. The storm is visibly brewing in the distance, but FIONN's immediate space is still and quiet.

STAGE PICTURE: FIONN is alone, holding a piece of discarded net—a symbol of his livelihood and his denial. The mood is reflective.

MUSIC CUE / ATMOSPHERE: A familiar, sea-worn folk melody returns, but the words and the feeling are no longer the same—FIONN sings it differently now. The music is sparse: acoustic guitar, perhaps a single mournful accordion or cello. The rhythm should be slow, acoustic, and simple—like a creaking boat at rest.

(The scene begins with FIONN singing the opening line of the revised melody.)

"A QUIET HARBOR"

FIONN
(Quietly, starting almost like a spoken reflection)
I built this life on silence.
A good boat needs no singing.
A safe man never asks
What the water keeps bringing.

Just net the fish, check the tide,
Don't listen to the whisper,
Don't worry 'bout the things you hide,

Just survive the next winter.

(A small shift in the music, becoming slightly more melodic.)

I wanted a quiet harbor.
No waves breaking the glass.
No argument from my neighbor,
Just the shadows when they pass.

I thought that quiet was control,
A sensible, solid plan.
The quickest way to save your soul
Is be a practical man.

(Bridge: The moment of realization - the Ache of Belonging. The music shifts, becoming slightly more melodic and vulnerable.)

But quiet isn't peace, is it?
Quiet is just a promise
That you'll forget what you miss,
And bury every solace.

I built a wall to keep her out,
And starved the part of me I doubt.

(Focuses on his building of the wall.)

I thought my life was running free,
A ship set out upon the sea.
But I just rode that rusted, sorry ride,
The Carousel of what I hid inside.

(Focuses on his acts of suppression.)

I drowned the songs, I buried deep,
The vows that I swore I would keep.

(The melody deepens, becoming slightly more open and tender.)

The ache of belonging,
The ache of letting go.
That's the only real longing
The old men ever know.

I shut the music out for years,
Pretended I was strong.
Now I hear the water's tears—
And they've been my song all along.

*(Final line, delivered with a sense of broken acceptance
and tenderness, looking at the net.)*

The quiet harbor... it was just a cage.

*(Music fades immediately into the sustained low HUM
of the sea's heartbeat, leading directly into the emotional
and physical reveal of the plot twist.)*

SCENE 8

Sea You Later (Reprise)

SETTING: The Harbor Docks area. The storm has paused.

STAGE PICTURE: The stage glows with soft, unnatural bioluminescent light. The broken nets from Act One drift across the set like ghosts. FIONN stands center stage, soaked and exhausted.

CHARACTER ACTION: From the heavy mist, LÍ BAN re-emerges, her cloak restored and her presence stronger than before, signaling the true confrontation.

(The scene begins as LÍ BAN steps out of the mist.)

FIONN

I held onto this cloak like a man holding his breath. I thought I could outrun the water.

LÍ BAN

And did you?

FIONN

Only myself.

LÍ BAN
(Looking past FIONN, toward the rising mist where MUIRGEN will later appear, her voice taking on a profound tone.)

I was always just the surface, Fionn. The turning is what matters now.

"SEA YOU LATER (REPRISE)"

FIONN
(Verse 1)
I kept your cloak, like a fool keeps a secret.
Though if I held on, I'd stop the tide.
I built a wall out of fear and of timber,
But there's nowhere left for a coward to hide.

LÍ BAN
(Verse 1)
The painted horses have all stopped their turning,
The golden nets have all dissolved into grey.
You held the fabric while the harbor was burning,
But the salt has a way... of washing the winter away.

FIONN
Sea you later, maybe soon,
The sky forgot to hide the moon.
If you forgive the man I've been,
I'll learn to breathe the deep again.

LÍ BAN
Sea you later, maybe now,
You kept the promise, kept the vow.
The tide returns what love won't drown—
The sea remembers every sound.

(Bridge: The music swells-Warm Brass but soft, like a distant lighthouse.)

FIONN
(Verse 2)
I'll be the anchor that stays in the sand...

LÍ BAN
(Verse 3)
I'll be the waves as they reach for land...

BOTH
(harmonizing in a slow, heartbeat rhythm)

The surface is a mirror, but the depth is a door,
We aren't the people we were on the shore.
(Hold your breath…).
We aren't the shadows we were anymore.

BOTH
(Full harmony)

Sea you later, maybe soon,
The tide returns what love won't drown.
If we meet when hearts are clear,
Hold your breath—I'm always near.

(Outro: Sea birds and soft harp)

Sea you later…
Sea you later…

(They touch foreheads; faint shimmer of light between them—then dissolve into the next song "What Remains When We Stop Blaming.")

SCENE 9

The Unsettled Tab

SETTING: The Wrecked Docks, following the initial flood.

STAGE PICTURE: Only FIONN and MUIRGEN (LÍ BAN) remain on stage. The scene is illuminated by the faint bioluminescent glow from the sea. The nets drift upward now, like memories unthreading—a potent visual metaphor of release.

MUSIC CUE / ATMOSPHERE: The final measure of "Sea You Later (Reprise)" hangs on the word 'near', sustained on strings. The harmony does not resolve; instead, a single cello note slides downward, and the tempo slows. The scene is an intimate 6/8 ballad sung by FIONN and MUIRGEN.

CHARACTER ACTION: LÍ BAN gently releases FIONN's hands. He then looks toward MUIRGEN's silhouette/shadow, which hovers faintly behind a scrim of mist—watching, not yet intervening. The underscore continues beneath the final line of dialogue / lyrics.

(Dialogue lead-in)

FIONN
(Softly, taking a steadying breath. This is the truth he found in his solo.)

The sea and I—we've an unsettled tab.

MUIRGEN
(The shadow speaks, profound and sad.)

You finally saw it—your world unmade by its own comfort. Do you still call that mercy?

FIONN

Maybe mercy's just the tide turning slow enough for fools to notice.

(*MUIRGEN studies him. He is soaked, shaking, honest for once.*)

(*Dialogue Bridge*)

(*MUIRGEN steps forward into the light, human-scaled now, no wings. She moves closer to FIONN, her hand reaching toward his chest. The low HUM subtly rises in volume.*)

(*The low, sustained HUM / HEARTBEAT continues. FIONN is exhausted and reeling from the CLERK's revelation and his own solo. He is broken. The tone is profound, sad remembrance.*)

FIONN
(*Voice cracking. He flinches, the pragmatic habit dying hard as he gestures wildly at the rising water.*)

I don't know what you want. A speech? An apology? I can't plug a thousand leaks with a sorry, Muirgen. If you want it to stop, tell me what to do!

MUIRGEN
(*Her voice is not accusatory, but profound and sad. She moves closer, her hand reaching toward his chest.*)

You keep asking me what I want, Fionn Murchadh. You've forgotten how to ask yourself.

(*The low HUM subtly rises in volume.*)

FIONN
(*The truth hitting him like a physical blow.*)

I just wanted... a life. A quiet harbor. I wanted survival.

MUIRGEN
(*Softly, the Whisper Melody returns, intertwining with the HUM. She holds the glowing net up between them.*)

You wanted the songs you silenced. The tenderness you traded for survival. This net... it isn't the sea's grief, it's the shape of your silence. I was the memory you bottled up inside the boat. I was the ache of belonging, the one you had to cast out to keep living. You hid your own coat.

FIONN

(A broken whisper of recognition. He looks down, acknowledging his guilt and his lost self.)

Muirgen…

(He finally sees her as his Anima, his Nature.)

You're not the tide. You're the turn. The heart I left behind.

(The lights shift completely, fusing the two figures in a single, intense beam, symbolizing the psychological fusion of the Anima and Animus.)

(FIONN collapses to his knees under the weight of this realization and guilt, fueling toward a song of action.)

(The sound design swells slightly, The HUM joined by a deep cello note—a sound of acceptance.)

FIONN
(To MUIRGEN's shadow)

You were right. I heard every wave, but not the cry beneath it. I'm done running from the sound, Muirgen. I'm staying until the heartbeat is the only thing left.

MUIRGEN

You heard yourself. That's all the sea ever asked.

(She steps forward into light—human-scaled now, no wings.)

[Muirgen and Lí Ban are technically different "aspects" of the same force, and so, Lí Ban's is also physically present. When Muirgen says "He already has," and then transitions into the song, Fionn isn't just talking to a ghost—he's reconciling with the very nature of the sea.]

LÍ BAN
(The Selkie, urging the goddess)

Then let him go.

MUIRGEN

He already has.

> *(MUIRGEN gestures; the harp picks up a slow ¾
> rhythm, shimmering major-minor ambiguity—the
> heartbeat evolved.)*

"WHAT REMAINS WHEN WE STOP BLAMING"

MUIRGEN
(Verse 1)

I weighed the storms, I counted tears,
Built my throne from all your fears.
But fear's a mirror, never true—
It shows the hurt, not what to do.

FIONN
(Verse 2)

I blamed the tide, I blamed the rain,
I blamed the sea to hide my pain.
But blame's a rope that pulls you down—
Cut it loose and you won't drown.

MUIRGEN
(Harmony with LÍ BAN)

Let the current find its way,
Let the dark be light today.

> *(The stage lighting warms from indigo to rose-gold; the
> storm stills. Feathers drift like snow.)*

BOTH

What remains when we stop blaming?
Only breath. Only light reclaiming.
If the sea forgives, then so can we—
What remains is love, and memory.

ENSEMBLE
(Enters softly from edges)
What remains when we stop blaming?
Water turns to grace in naming.
Every drop becomes a song,
Calling home the hearts gone wrong.

FIONN

I built my pride from rope and rust,
A net of doubt, a web of dust.
I blamed the storm for what I broke,
And swallowed guilt until I choked.

MUIRGEN

I counted crimes in mortal tones,
Till mercy calcified to stones.
But every wave that touched your fear
Sang back the truth I'd failed to hear.

BOTH

What remains when we stop blaming?
Only breath. Only light reclaiming.
If the sea forgives, then so can we—
What remains is love, and memory.

*(They move in mirrored steps; a soft current of light
sweeps between them.)*

MUIRGEN

Go back to them, Fionn. The sea is tired of punishment.

FIONN

And you?

MUIRGEN

I'll rest when the silence hums again.

*(She dissolves into a swirl of feathers and mist; the faint
melody of "The Ocean Remembers" begins underneath.)*

"THE OCEAN REMEMBERS"

(Begins almost a Capella, then grows to full-company swell.)

*(A golden wash breaks through blue; chaos quiets
toward dawn.)*

*(Ensemble gathers debris and arranges it into a spiral
pattern. Each object glows softly as harmony builds.)*

*(Sound begins with a single heartbeat, then is layered
with vocal drones. It ends with a final major-key
resolution on the word "remembers.")*

ENSEMBLE

The ocean remembers the shape of your name,
Though you buried it deep in the silt of shame.
She hums in the shells, in the bones of the quay—
Forgive her, forgive you, let it be.

We cast our nets not for profit but peace,
We mend what we tore, we grant release.
The gulls take flight, the horizon bends,
The sea forgets nothing—but she mends.

Oh tide, oh turning, cradle of sky,
Lift every bottle, let memory dry.
What drowns may rise, what spoils may heal,
The ocean remembers—so we will feel.

MUIRGEN
(final line; floats over the rising music.)
I am not the end, but the air that stays
Forgive yourselves, and the sea obeys.

(Pause—silence—heartbeat resumes in distant drums.)

(The music swells briefly.)

SCENE 10

Storm of Mercy

SETTING: The Harbor Stage.

LIGHTING / ATMOSPHERE: The entire stage is dramatically awash in cobalt and gold. Rain and wind are projected as rhythmic, stylized pulses, achieving a thematic, non-realistic effect.

STAGE PICTURE: MUIRGEN appears center stage, her cloak spread wide. FIONN faces her, holding the feather in his hand, ready for the confrontation.

(They sing the opening verse.)

"STORM OF MERCY"

FIONN
You asked for books to balance right,
I brought a heart too full to write.

MUIRGEN
Then pay in kindness, not in coin—
Let mercy be the line we join.

(She touches the feather; lightning freezes mid-air, transforming into beams of light.)

CHORUS
(COMPANY enters)
Storm of mercy, break and mend,
Wash us clean, begin again!
What was curse becomes design,
Dark and gold in equal line.

(Crow Chorus swoop, scattering feathers like snow.)

(LÍ BAN lifts the net; it gleams with starlight instead of fish.)

(Bridge - BANSHEE & MINISTER OF FLOW)

BANSHEE

You promise no more empty spin?

MINISTER OF FLOW

I wait until the truth sinks in!

(They laugh, joining hands, comic-romantic redemption.)

CHORUS *(Final Refrain - Full Company)*
Storm of mercy, sing us through,
Every tide a chance to renew!
What we broke, we choose to heal—
The ocean remembers, the love is real!

(Thunder softens to birdsong. Lighting shifts from blue to rose dawn.)

SCENE 11

Coda: Oh Shite, It's Real (Reprise)

SETTING: The Docks.

STAGE PICTURE: The light is soft and hazy, signaling that the crisis is visually past. The ENSEMBLE is still present, dramatically frozen in the stage position from the last scene.

MUSIC CUE / ATMOSPHERE: The low HUM of the mythic scenes has been replaced by the jaunty, jig-worthy melody of the "Oh Shite" reprise. The musical cue is the upbeat, sardonic melody of "Oh Shite, It's Real" returning in 6/8.

(The scene begins as the Ensemble breaks their freeze and launches into the Coda.)

HARBORMASTER
(Breaks the freeze, speaks directly to the audience, deadpan.)

Minutes from the final meeting: Planet—survived by its sense of humor.

(The BANSHEE and MINISTER OF FLOW break the freeze, and the full ENSEMBLE launches into the short, energetic reprise, tapping buckets and debris like percussion.)

———————————————

"OH SHITE, IT'S REAL (REPRISE)"

BANSHEE
(Belts out with full dramatic flair)
Oh shite, it's real, the sea can smile!
The pipes don't spew in graceful style!

(Buckets become percussion; audience claps along.)

MINISTER OF FLOW / CLERK

(Trying to sound official)

We'll file reports in triplicate,
Regarding this change in ecological fate!

CROW CHORUS

(Swooping with a final, ironic flourish)

The gulls are back, the air is clean,
Now who's going to pay for this new regime?

(The entire COMPANY takes a single, unified step forward.)

TAG-COMIC CALL-AND-RESPONSE ENSEMBLE

ENSEMBLE

What did we learn?

BANSHEE

(Leads the final shout to the audience, brass flourish.)

Oh shite, be real!
*(The music cuts short one final time, leaving the townspeople laughing—
but the laughter immediately dissolves as the final image begins.)*

(Tag-Comic Call-and-Response)

ENSEMBLE

What did we learn?

AUDIENCE *(led by BANSHEE)*

Oh shite, be real!

(Big laugh, brass flourish.)

FINAL IMAGE

The Net of Light

SETTING: The Docks.

MUSIC CUE / LIGHTING: The raucous laughter from the Coda immediately dissolves as the final image begins. All sound falls away except a single, very low HUM—the same sea heartbeat from "Listen." The lighting shifts to an impossibly slow, deep rose-gold DAWN.

STAGE PICTURE / SYMBOLISM: The rusted frame that defined the set is gone. In its place, a shimmering, full CAROUSEL structure now stands. It is not cheap or garish but built of gleaming brass, wood, and light, reflecting the dawn. The painted horses are replaced by mythical sea creatures—dolphins, selkies, and whales—all waiting, still. It is a symbol of potential joy and renewal, not yet running.

CHARACTER ACTION: FIONN stands alone at the waterline (center stage), holding the NET OF GOLDEN FEATHERS—the transformed net from Scene 10. He gently throws the repaired net back toward the sea. LÍ BAN, positioned near the waterline, receives the net. She raises it slowly and reverently. It is transformed, a visual metaphor that is filled with shimmering light and rising feathers (no catch, just light). The net continues to ascend silently into the fly space. Crows circle overhead, with golden feathers falling like soft snow over the scene.

MUIRGEN *(her voice only)*
(A pure, whispered melody, overlapping the rising net.)

Balance restored. Memory kept.

(The ENSEMBLE re-enters, walking slowly in a circular, reverent path, unifying behind FIONN and LÍ Ban, facing the dawn. They are still, accepting the quiet. This slow, unifying movement represents the completed "Carousel" cycle.)

(Instrumental Rise)

COMPANY **/** ENSEMBLE

(They breathe together once—a long, slow, shared, silent inhale, then exhale.)

"THE NET OF LIGHT"

COMPANY **/** ENSEMBLE

The net of light returns to sea,
No catch of bone, only memory.
Feathers fall where sorrow lay,
The wheel of tides turns joy's new day.

(Choir – gentle waltz)
Round we stand in quiet grace,
Dawn arrives, the sea's embrace.
Not yet spinning, still, made whole,
Carousel of mended soul.
(Choir – very soft)
What was taken now returns,
Sea remembers, sea discerns.
Hands once closed now open wide,
We walk forward with the tide.

(The stage dissolves into sunrise. The light holds. Silence, save for a single, final sound.)

(A single, final, deep BASS DRUM beat—steady, whole—the settled heartbeat of the sea.)

(The WALTZ / CALLIOPE motif rises, clear and joyful. A single light reveals the center pole of the new CAROUSEL. It does not turn.)

(Instrumental Calliope Waltz)

(Harp and distant calliope. Crows cry.)

(The light holds for a slow, long beat. The CAROUSEL turns once more as the light widens, then GENTLY fades on a single sustained note of harp and the soft cry of crows.)

(Deep Bass Drum)

(One final heartbeat.)

(The sea HUM remains, steady and whole.)

CURTAIN

APPENDIX

The Cloak as Mythic Symbol

Now that you have completed the journey of Fionn and Lí Ban, this essay outlines the structural and thematic logic that guided the creation of the work. The central mythic object of the musical—the Selkie cloak belonging to the Child of the Sea, Lí Ban—is not merely a plot device, but the Thematic Engine of the entire work.

1. The Genesis of the Cloak: Synchronicity and Craft

The central mythic object of *Muirgen's Carousel*—the Selkie cloak belonging to the Child of the Sea, Lí Ban—emerged from an unplanned moment of magical synchronicity.

The physical object—a handmade hooded jacket created by the author from sustainable, hand-knit netting with an intricately embroidered exterior—was already a vessel for the play's core themes years before the script was written. The embroidery on the surface tells a small yet complete narrative: Two twin fish are caught in a fisherman's net, and their friends bite the threads to free them.

The twin fish, trapped by human industry, became the symbolic representation of Fionn's drowned brother (trauma) and Lí Ban's trapped spirit (the wound). Both are victims of the net of exploitation.

The friends biting the nets became the ultimate image of collective sacrifice and the breaking of the cycle of exploitation, the exact redemption Fionn achieves in Act Two.

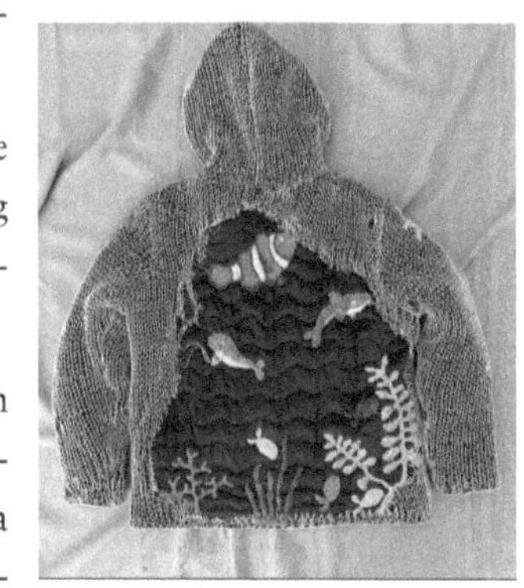

The fact that this deeply personal "story on cloth" manifested as the play's central symbolic object confirms the material arose from a place of deep, intuitive craft and spiritual connection, grounding the abstract ecological message in a tangible, artisanal truth.

2. Defining the Function: Engine, Not Plot Device

In a musical rooted in myth and collective redemption, the Selkie cloak is not a plot device. It functions as the thematic engine and the most powerful mythic symbol in the play, physically anchoring the abstract ecological message.

A. The Cloak as Thematic Engine: A Study in Autonomy

The cloak is the physical representation of Lí Ban's Autonomy and Connection to Nature. Its state on stage directly reflects humanity's moral state:

The initial Loss or Theft of the cloak symbolizes Humanity's Control over Nature. This act represents the historic moment when humanity (like the Fisherman who originally traps her) severed the natural world's right to freedom and exploited it for human comfort or survival. The cloak's absence is the central metaphor for the town's collective guilt.

Conversely, the cloak's Restoration and Transformation signify the Restoration of Balance (Reverence). This return, which is catalyzed by Fionn's sacrifice of the Net of Oppression in Act One, symbolizes the necessary reversal of that original transgression. The message is clear: the natural world can truly heal only when humanity gives back autonomy.

B. The Cloak as Mythic Symbol: From Trauma to Grace

The cloak, and its final form—the Net of Light—is the visible link between Fionn's internal, personal guilt and the sea's mythic, environmental wound.

The plot utilizes the cloak for two critical, symbolic actions:

- Act One Climax (Sacrifice): Fionn performs the physical act of abandoning his net—the Net of Oppression—with Lí Ban's cloak tangled in it. This action is the literal sacrificing of his livelihood and his guilt, proving he is ready to restore autonomy.

- Act Two Climax (Forgiveness): Lí Ban / Muirgen accepts Fionn's sacrifice, and the cloak is transformed into the Net of Golden Feathers (Scene 11). This is not a net for catching; it is a symbol filled only with light, representing grace and renewed potential.

Conclusion: The cloak is essential. Its fate is the play's fate, moving from being an object of trauma to a vessel of forgiveness. It proves that the play is about the spiritual choice of giving back autonomy, rather than simply paying a debt.

Author's Note on Staging and Form

This document is a structural blueprint for the musical, *Muirgen's Carousel*. The flow, rhythmic shifts, and sequencing of emotional beats are designed based on a specific psychological approach to audience engagement.

To achieve the Intended Effect of transitioning the audience from denial (Act One) to confrontation and acceptance (Act Two), certain moments must be precisely executed to trigger the correct cognitive and emotional responses.

Therefore, the following notes detail the Mandatory Structural and Thematic Goals, Prescribed Actions, and Core Rhythmic Foundations for every scene. Adherence to these structural beats ensures the narrative's psychological persuasive arc is maintained and delivered as intended.

Prelude: The Ocean Remembers

This Prelude is structurally vital as it establishes the mythic wound and sets the moral stakes. The emotional arc must transition clearly from sacred, then mournful, then hopeful ("wake, rise, set it free"), creating the thematic appetite for the action that follows. The core rhythmic foundation is the slow 6/8 heartbeat motif (low drone / sub-bass frequency) that will anchor the entire play. The emotional layering must be preserved: reverent sorrow, then eerie stillness, then boisterous denial. The "Carousel Wakes" beat is the critical pivot, shifting the world from mythic timelessness to the modern town. The soundscape must shift from the sustained whale drone to the realistic, metallic creaking of the Carousel, accelerating the shift into the human world.

Act One: Descent into Denial

Scene 1: What's One More Drop?

The structural purpose is to establish the town's state of collective denial through cynicism and energetic distraction immediately. The rhythmic goal is a busy, ironic pace (overlapping dialogue, comic momentum) to maximize the potency of the later stillness. The Banshee Wail must be the first sound of the suffering ocean that shocks and interrupts the town's cynical rhythm. The silence immediately following the high-energy song must feel full of listening, forcing focus onto the sound design. The low, subtle sub-bass frequency (The HUM / Heartbeat) must enter the soundscape, creating the rhythmic foundation of foreboding, which the Crow Chorus signposts with their action and dialogue.

Scene 2: The Net Is Empty

This short scene shifts focus from collective denial to the protagonist's personal conflict, linking Fionn's private guilt to the town's communal disease. Fionn actively chooses the "wry shanty" as a defense mechanism against the truth. The low HUM (the sea's heartbeat) must be sustained beneath the music's quietest points to provide rhythmic contrast to his deflection. The scene must visually foreshadow the plot by including the feather moment, a recommended structural motif that anticipates Lí Ban and the "Net of Light."

Scene 3: Sea You Later

This is the Inciting Encounter, the hinge moment where the story slips from the mundane to the mythic. The tone must balance warm, whimsical banter with a clear existential threat / dread. The 6/8 heartbeat motif (low HUM) must be sustained beneath the dialogue. The score must transition from a lilting jig (banter) to a softer 6/8 waltz (memory / romantic high point). The climax is the Cloak Action: Lí Ban must rapidly shed the shimmering cloak, ensuring it is visibly caught in Fionn's net—the new emotional anchor that drives the plot into Act Two.

Scene 4: Forms in Triplicate

This scene provides necessary comic release, serving as the thematic mirror where bureaucracy equals human denial. Staging must be a highly choreographed physical comedy utilizing desks and paper as visual percussion. The rhythm must be a comedic pressure cooker, escalating quickly into a double-tempo patter song to achieve maximum absurdity. The score should be a percussive farce, including a rhythmic echo to link administrative denial back to the Prelude's theme of "drops." The scene ends with a precise technical cue: Lightning flicker, decisive thunder cut, abrupt music cut, leaving the final image of papers scattering like snow.

Scene 5: Progress Afloat

This is the large-ensemble showstopper that acts as the structural anchor of false victory. It must explode immediately after the bureaucratic farce to create maximum momentum contrast. The score is an ironic brass-band sound ("Sousa-meets-klezmer"), utilizing a call-and-response rhythm to emphasize collective, mindless consent. Bunting, banners, and twirling paperwork must be used as a visual motif for future debris. The dialogue exchange about "Muirgen's Carousel" is a recommended beat, anchoring the theme of cyclical denial. The scene ends with a precise sequence: Music cuts mid-trumpet note, with the Crow Chorus whisper, "Caw... audit incoming."

Scene 6: Muirgen's First Omen

This is the transitional vision that creates the first fracture between laughter and awe, the shiver before intermission. The pacing must maintain a speed that creates unease. The brass band must fade out in slow motion until only the hiss of wind remains. The low HUM (part cello, part wind) begins to pulse, establishing the "heartbeat" connection. Muirgen's voice must be amplified / offstage to suggest a non-human presence. Her speech is a direct audit, linking the town's administrative denial to her spiritual accounting. The final focus must be on Fionn's isolated action (catching the feather), which is the final visual before the Blackout.

Scene 7: Why I Don't Swim

This is the core scene that defines Fionn's internal, mythic conflict ("The sea and I—we've an unsettled tab"). The pub atmosphere, loud and cynical, must constantly contrast with and threaten the intimate conversation between Fionn and Lí Ban. The scene must stage the mythic ambiguity of Lí Ban's presence (potentially only visible to Fionn), though the Banshee must provide the only external validation. The phrase "The sea and I—we've an unsettled tab" is a recommended foreshadowing device.

Scene 8: Pints and Plastic

This scene acts as the emotional hinge of Act One, moving rapidly from Raucous Shanty to Fionn's Soft Reflection, then Manic Singalong, then Communal Dread. The final song, "Oh Shite... It's Real," must be performed at maximum manic energy and a doubled tempo to mask the town's fear. The Banshee's sharp interruption, where the music cuts and the faint underwater heartbeat motif returns, is the key rhythmic pivot. Fionn's private guilt must be revealed visually by furtively touching the feather. The Blackout must be instantaneous after the Banshee's final, soft line ("She's already in").

SCENE 9: INTERLUDE — THE STORM REMEMBERS

This is the short, essential Transitional Vision / Trauma Flashback. The soundscape must be highly specific: laughter dissolves, then surf, then a low, sustained heartbeat drum swells into waves. The gull cry must transform into deafening thunder. Minimal staging, maximum visual impact: utilize a blue-grey wash with light strobing during the drowning moment. The offstage voice of the Child of the Sea delivers the core psychological revelation: "You kept my storm inside you." The transition is anchored by Fionn's quiet exhale and the single bubble of light rising.

SCENE 10: THE AUDIT OF SOULS / "BALANCE THE BOOKS" (ACT ONE CLIMAX)

This is the Act One Climax and Mythic Reckoning—the final, massive collision. The stage must visually represent a collapse: walls peel away to reveal dark water and lightning. The abstraction of policy failure must manifest as physical catastrophe—visually represented by a gush of brown water shooting up from a pipe fracture. Muirgen's arrival must be a non-costumed spectacle: revealed in mist, illuminated by lightning flashes. The chorus song must quote the original "What's One More Drop?" melody, slowed and in a minor key, transforming irony into audible judgment. Fionn's final action is his confession and the crucial act of leaving the net with Lí Ban's cloak tangled in it. The Blackout is followed by absolute silence for one beat, then the low HUM of the heartbeat must continue faintly (the auditory thread leading to Act Two).

ACT TWO: RECKONING AND RENEWAL

SCENE 1: WHAT FLOATS?

This scene is the Act Two opener and the Chaos Sequence, providing necessary comic relief while showing the literal fallout of the policy failure. STAGING: The set must be visibly damaged and slick with water, with lighting using brown-gold ripples through mist. The choreography must be slapstick (slipping, flailing). MANDATORY GAG: The floating garden gnome must punctuate the final beat of the dance break. The ensemble song must be a chaotic patter and must include a clear comic tango echo in the bridge. The scene transitions with Fionn and Lí Ban plunging offstage.

SCENE 2: YOU PROMISE / I WAIL

This is the Comic Tango Duet, immediately relieving tension while providing a political / rhythmic pivot. Mops and microphones are mandatory props, doubling as tango aids and symbolic extensions of their roles. The music must be a distinct tango vamp, shifting from aggressive patter to bittersweet vulnerability. The choreography must be a half-embrace, half-stalemate. The dance break is key: Banshee must use the mop to flick dirty water toward the Minister of Flow's shoes ("truth stains silk"). The scene ends on a visual of mutual failure.

SCENE 3: COUNCIL OF MYTHS

This scene provides the Comic Debate and Rhythmic Reset. The set must be visibly half-submerged, demanding creative staging so actors can use the water for slapstick. The central song is a rapid-fire comic patter ("Guilt by the Gallon"). The scene hinges on Fionn's transformation cue: his line, "Look at us— arguing while the sea's still in the room," must create a sudden, shared silence (Beat of Stillness).

SCENE 4: GUILT BY THE GALLON (REPRISE) -TRANSITION

This is the Tone Bridge that seamlessly converts the frantic comic energy into a quiet, reflective space. The music must quote the patter song but transform it: half-tempo, minor-key, and wistful. The music must pause explicitly with the rhythm of water dripping. The final visual is the lighting shift from the harsh amber of the council meeting to a soft silver wash, isolating Fionn.

SCENE 5: HEART OF THE SEA VISION (THE CHILD)

This is the Quiet, Mystical Centerpiece. The stage must empty into near-darkness, revealing a childlike glow (translucent blue) from beneath the water. The soundscape is defined by the low heartbeat, then distant whale calls, then a single harp string plucked repeatedly ("Listen"). As Fionn kneels, concentric circles must ripple outward (projection). The Child's voice must be an ethereal soprano. The final whispered line is: "She's waiting to forgive herself too."

SCENE 6: THE CLERK'S FEAR (THE COMPLICITY CRISIS)

This is the Dramatic Spike that forces Fionn into concrete, personal guilt. The Clerk's presence must be frantic and bureaucratic. The core reveal is his line: "They used your silence as their signature," elevating Fionn's failure to active complicity. The Clerk drops the saturated binder and runs off, and the shock must immediately transition into Fionn's solo.

SCENE 7: THE QUIET HARBOR (FISHERMAN'S SOLO)

This is the Internal Low Point and realization that Fionn's survival strategy was actually a cage. The score must be sparse and acoustic, maintaining a slow rhythm like a creaking boat. Fionn must be holding the discarded net throughout. The mandatory lyric callback to the Carousel motif proves Fionn's journey has circled back to confront his truth ("But I just rode that rusted, sorry ride...."). The music must fade immediately into the sustained low HUM of the sea's heartbeat.

SCENE 8: SEA YOU LATER (REPRISE)

This scene functions as the Emotional Bridge and Duet of Recognition. The staging must be minimal and mystical: soft bioluminescent light and mist with the broken nets visible. The core physical action is the touch of foreheads with a faint shimmer of light. Musically, the reprise restores the core 6/8 rhythm (slower, minor key). Lí Ban's final line—"The turning is what matters now"—is the key transition. The scene dissolves directly into the next with no blackout.

SCENE 9: THE UNSETTLED TAB / ANIMA FUSION AND FORGIVENESS (CLIMAX)

This is the Climactic Revelation and Duet of Collective Grace. The transition must be a deceleration (cello note slides downward). The core moment is the Anima Fusion, physicalized by the lights fusing Fionn and Muirgen in a single, intense beam upon his realization ("You're the turn."). Fionn's collapse to his knees is mandatory. The Ensemble enters softly, and feathers drifting like snow serve as the visual metaphor for grace. The Ensemble arranges debris into a glowing spiral pattern. The scene ends with a final Pause—silence, followed by the heartbeat resuming in distant drums.

Scene 10: Storm of Mercy (Collective Redemption)

This is the Collective Redemption Crescendo and the highest energy musical moment. The stage must be intensely lit, awash in cobalt and gold, with rain and wind projected as rhythmic pulses. The symbolic action is crucial: Muirgen touches the feather, and lightning freezes mid-air, transforming into beams of light. Lí Ban lifts the net, which must gleam with starlight. This must be the high-energy crescendo, fusing all musical themes. The sound must cut abruptly at the conclusion, leaving a brief, shocking silence.

Scene 11: Coda: Oh Shite, It's Real (Reprise), then Final Image

The Coda provides the Comic Epilogue at the highest comedic energy. The transition to the Final Image is achieved by a ruthless cut to silence and the single, very low HUM (sea heartbeat). The stage reveals an impossibly slow, deep rose-gold DAWN and the completed Carousel structure, which does not yet turn (symbol of choice). Fionn's final act is deliberate and slow, as he gently throws the NET OF GOLDEN FEATHERS back toward the sea. The Ensemble re-enters slowly, tracing a circular, reverent path (completing the cycle). The final sound is a single, deep BASS DRUM beat (settled heartbeat) and the WALTZ / CALLIOPE motif rising.

Sound Designer's Note:

The HUM (approx. 40–60 Hz) should be felt as much as heard, acting as the connective tissue between the mythic Prelude and the human Reckoning.

Glossary of Terms

Banshee *(Irish: "Woman of the Fairy Mound")*: A female spirit whose wail traditionally signals death; in this work, a spectral figure embodying collective, ignored grief and a source of comic-operatic commentary.

Fionn Murchadh *(Irish: "Fair Warrior / Sea-Warrior")*: The protagonist, a fisherman struggling with self-imposed emotional exile.

Lí Ban *(Irish: "Woman of Beauty / Sea-Water")*: A Selkie figure, the human-scaled embodiment of the sea's compassion and the lost love of Fionn.

Minister of Flow: The satirical title for a local politician concerned with maintaining the flow of bureaucracy and narrative control rather than solving the ecological crisis.

Muirgen *(Irish: "Sea-born")*: The sea personified; an ancient goddess and the elemental aspect of Lí Ban.

Muirgen's Carousel: The central symbolic image of the play: a rusted, half-submerged amusement ride representing a beautiful but broken cycle, the denial of memory, and the potential for renewal.

Selkie: A mythological creature from Celtic folklore that resembles a seal in the water but can shed its skin to walk on land as a human.

Performance Rights and Licensing

Caution: Professionals and amateurs are hereby warned that *Muirgen's Carousel: The Hope of Return* is subject to royalty. It is fully protected under the copyright laws of the United States of America, the British Commonwealth, including the Dominion of Canada, and all other countries of the Copyright Union.

The right of performance is strictly reserved.

No performance, reading, workshop, recording, or broadcast (whether televised, online, or streamed) of this work may be given without the express written permission of the author.

Dramatic Integrity Clause: All casting, scenic design, musical arrangements, and alterations to the text or score must be submitted to and approved in writing by M. Turandot.

Musical Rights: Performance royalty payments for the full work must be satisfied with both the librettist and the composer. Inquiries regarding the musical score should be directed to the librettist at the address above pending formal composer credit and PRO registration.

Inquiries: For all performance, recording, and licensing inquiries, please contact: M. Turandot joycanvasstudios@gmail.com.

Acknowledgments

My deepest gratitude goes to my surgeon father, Dr. Cevdet Turan, whose stories of attending Broadway musicals during his postgraduate work in New York City (1959–1961) first instilled in me a lifelong love for the language of song and story.

This work is indebted to the creative spirits who taught me that the highest drama often lies in the most resonant song. My structural and musical ambitions owe a profound debt to the genius of the American Theatre tradition, particularly the thematic bravery and elegant construction of Rodgers and Hammerstein and to the theatrical legends, Alan Jay Lerner and Frederick Loewe, whose brilliant creative synergy, combined lush, beguiling melodies with witty, character-driven, sophisticated lyrics and books. The central 6/8 "heartbeat" motif was inspired by the music of *Brigadoon*.

My heartfelt gratitude also goes to my family for their unwavering support and patience throughout this journey.

I am indebted to the bravery of those documenting the crisis of our oceans. Specifically, the visceral footage of bottom trawling in *Ocean (2025)* and the critical, in-depth analysis of fishing practices in *Seaspiracy (2021)* provided the necessary, stark foundation for this fictional world.

Thank you to all the early readers and supporters who encouraged me to find the music in the silence.

This is for the ones who listen.

About the Author

M. TURANDOT is an author, artist, and storyteller whose work integrates mythic narrative with psychological insights. *Muirgen's Carousel* grew from a lifelong engagement with folklore, theatre, and ecological imagination.

Based on the historic shores of Manakin-Sabot, Virginia—a landscape defined by both industrial legacy and natural resilience—Turandot explores the intersection of human grief and ecological restoration. *Muirgen's Carousel* represents the culmination of years of intuitive craft, from the hand-netted embroidery of its central symbols to a deep investigation of the cognitive rhythms that move an audience from denial to grace.

This edition of *Muirgen's Carousel* was set in Sabon, a face designed by Jan Tschichold in 1964. It was composed by the author on the shores of a lake in Manakin-Sabot, Virginia.